FUTUREMAN
DAVID AVIDAN

Translated by Tsipi Keller

Introduction by Anat Weisman

PHONEME
MEDIA

Phoneme Media
P.O. BOX 411272
Los Angeles, CA 90041

First Edition, 2017

Hebrew language copyright © Tsiporen Lotem, 1964, 1973, 1974, 1980, 1985, 1991.
English language translation copyright © Tsipi Keller 2017.
Introduction copyright © Anat Weisman 2017.

ISBN: 978-1-944700-14-0

This book is distributed by Publishers Group West

Cover image: copyright © 1981
David Avidan in Message from the Future (MFF Productions)
by permission of Tsiporen Lotem

Cover design and typesetting by Jaya Nicely

All rights reserved. Except for brief passages quoted for review purposes,
no part of this book may be reproduced in any form or by any means,
without permission in writing from the Publisher.

Phoneme Media is a nonprofit media company dedicated to promoting
cross-cultural understanding, connecting people and ideas
through translated books and films.

http://phonememedia.org

Curious books for curious people.

FUTUREMAN

CONTENTS

Introduction: **David Avidan: The Sadosemantic Poet**

*From **Something for Somebody—Selected Poems 1952-1964***
(Schocken, 1964)

From **Practical Poems** (The Thirtieth Century,
Levin-Epstein Modan, 1973)

From **The Book of Possibilities: Poems and More**
(Keter Publishing House, 1985)

From **The Latest Gulf** (Tirosh, 1991)

Poems Translated by the Poet

From **Cryptograms from a Telestar** (The Thirtieth Century, 1980)

From **My Electronic Psychiatrist—Eight Authentic Talks with a Computer** (Levin-Epstein Modan, 1974)

David Avidan :
The Sadosemantic Poet

David Avidan was born in Tel Aviv where he lived and worked. And yet, he didn't consider himself a Tel Aviv poet, but rather a galactic one. In an interview he gave while shooting his futuristic film *Message from the Future* (1981) Avidan proclaimed: "My arena is the entire planet. […] Israel is but a small piece of land. I don't work in Tel Aviv. I work from Tel Aviv." The film, one of Avidan's most grandiose projects—shot in English, German, Japanese, Russian, Hebrew, and French—proved a commercial and artistic flop, but, years later, especially in the last decade, it is occasionally screened in festivals and cinémathèques in Israel, and is mentioned in various forums. It is also a testimonial to the ambitious, but ultimately unsuccessful, attempt by the most avant-garde and experimental poet in the history of Hebrew poetry to get off the page.

Vito Acconci, the New York artist, described his transition from poetry to performance and video art in the sixties: "Once I realized I was so interested in movement, it seemed unnecessary to restrict that movement to an 8.5-by-11 piece of paper. There is a whole world out there or at least a street." Avidan, whose poetic ethos is kinetic, and whose work embodies movement in time, also attempted to get off the page in favor of more physical and utilitarian venues like the cinema, theater, and the visual arts, but his medium was and remains, first and foremost, the art of the word. His poetry is where his most compelling, individualistic experiments are rendered: his attempts to create movement in words, always combating the finality of the page.

Eventually, the film *Message from the Future* went back to the page as a poem (see page 135), and Avidan remained and remains "adamila" ("wordman")—just one of the many compound words he coined—and the poem on his gravestone reads: "The word I was / the word I will be / the word I was / before my birth / the word I will be after my death / the word that was in me / the word that is with me."

Born in 1934—the year Israel's National Poet, Hayim Nahman Bialik (1873, Ukraine), died in Tel Aviv—Avidan spent his childhood and early teens under the British Mandate. Tel Aviv was a small city along the Mediterranean Sea, built in eclectic architectural styles, combining European and Eastern elements. The dominant poetics was mostly Russian, and the poetry—romantic, melancholy, and suffused with nationalist longings—was in meter and rhyme. Poetry, in fact, was central in the life of the pre-state Yishuv, and poets, instrumental in the revival of Hebrew as a living language, were its cultural heroes. Soon, a new poetics would become dominant with the emergence of Nathan Alterman (1910, Warsaw – 1970, Tel Aviv) as the new hero and national poet. The linguistic virtuosity, the rhythms and vivid imagery of his first volume *Stars Outside* (1938) dazzled the Yishuv and marked a poetic turning point; when Avidan began his work as a poet, it was a generally accepted view that writing poetry meant writing "like Alterman."

Avidan's parents, who came from Eastern Europe, Hebraicized their last name from Moritz to Avidan. His mother was a homemaker, and his father, an engineer, worked at City Hall.

Asthmatic and an indifferent student, Avidan excelled in his favorite subject: Hebrew Language and Grammar. In an interview he gave in 1993, two years before his death, he spoke of his high school teacher, Haim Rosen (later, Professor of Linguistics at the Hebrew University of Jerusalem) with much gratitude and affection: "He taught me Hebrew. He taught me grammar. Basically, at the end of my first year I took and passed the "Bagrut"* exam in Grammar and so held an advantage over others, having acquired a driving license in Hebrew at age fifteen. And, at age sixteen, I became a good driver..."

Avidan's first poems appeared in 1951, in the literary pages of Israel's Communist journal *The Voice of the People*; the literary editor was the poet Alexander Penn, who translated into Hebrew the Cubo-Futurist-Communist poet Vladimir Mayakovski. Avidan was still a high school student when he joined the youth movement of the Party, and his very early poems were profoundly influenced by Mayakovski. Mayakovski continued to write and publish during the Stalin era, asserting that the Communist Party would provide the content, while the poet would concern himself with his métier: "word-making."

In later years, as Avidan's poetry turned toward other aesthetics and poetic experiments, Mayakovski's direct influence waned; still, Mayakovski's impact on Avidan's work and poetic persona remained relevant. In other words, when reading Avidan's poetry, one is well advised to bear in mind Mayakovski's futuristic-formalistic-radical concept of poetry and language, as opposed to an ideological-romantic-lyrical one. Additionally, Avidan, like Mayakovski, never tires of stressing that the foremost enemy of the poet is staticity, the daily routine, and he deploys the same symbolic means, sometimes soberly, at others, comically; their similar approach to immortality (always corporeal), their hostility to children who will fail to transform the future, their unique blend of a powerful expressive musicality and a consummate poet persona, very nearly renders these two poets spiritual twins.

Already in his early poems, Avidan's gift to imitate poetic models, to absorb literary influences in order to circumvent and reinvent them, is evident, and a few of the poems were included in Avidan's first volume *Lipless Faucets*. (The first six poems in *Futureman* are from *Lipless Faucets*.) Published in 1954, the year Avidan left the Party, it established Avidan as a Hebrew poet who could be ridiculed or vilified, but not ignored. Indeed, the title of one of the reviews that welcomed the book was "Why Blame the Faucets?"

One may read this first volume as a book that achieves the impossible: on the one hand, it offers a whimsical liquidation sale of poetry by mimicking other poets, a strategy that can be construed as both parodic and straightforward. For instance: "The Stain Remained on the Wall" (see page 27) is patterned on Berthold Brecht's "The Invincible Inscription" (1934); "Concerning the Gloomy Love of J. Alfred Prufrock" (see page 36) corresponds with T.S. Eliot's "Prufrock"; and "Interim Summation" explicitly relies on Alterman's volume *Stars Outside*. On the other hand, while making use of, and openly challenging, other poets' achievements, the twenty-year-old Avidan finds and creates his own voice. This voice would secure his position as a major Hebrew poet in the second half of the twentieth century, and a number of poems from this first book have since become iconic treasures.

But in Israel of the 1950s, *Lipless Faucets* was controversial from any conceivable angle: the brutal and sexual themes; the arrogant and misanthropic persona of the poet who abhors the collective; its odd and hybrid aesthetics; its cryptic surreal-apocalyptic visions; its existential and uncompromising bitterness; the absolute freedom from, and rejection of, communal values. For instance, the poem "Longterm Loathing" (see page 30), that begins:

> Ostensibly
> you loathe most of the folks
> who live with us and with you. Allofthem**
> one great foe and not very smart. Even
> the best of them—be wary

posits a new poetics, steeped in a strange and disjointed militant phraseology, and is delivered in one breath. Needless to say, the notions of battle, victory, and defeat, as expressed in the poem, did not accord with prevalent military ethos. The Avidanian war aims for radical individualism in a collective society, and its main weapon is humor, a humor that, like a double-edged sword, is also directed at its own aims. And, if he states in the poem that "you always/assume a militant stance" or that "Enmities/form the rare summits of your poetry"—Avidan ends the poem in his paradoxical, serious-droll fashion:

> The sun
> surveys the plane of the white heights
> with a nearly resigned look, as if
> once again she has endured a small defeat,
> a very small defeat, although
> the victory is a great one indeed.

Defeat? Victory? Both? In addition, this poem, conceivably, could continue forever in a kind of a verbal *perpetuum mobile*. Reviewers were quick to denounce the book in the press—attacking its author for being crude, arrogant, nihilistic, and clownish, and accusing him of mannerism, extravagance, and arbitrariness. (A letter to the editor, one of many, described Avidan's work as "a poetry wherein one may interchange words, lines, and even pages with impunity; one may even read the book backward, and a listener won't notice the difference.") Other reviews stressed and lamented the fact that the author and his book were symptomatic of a new generation that caricaturized values and ideals, thus revealing a sick attraction to nothingness, death, and chaos. They also condemned Avidan's linguistic virtuosity in deploying, in several of the poems, the poetic means and language of the admired poet Nathan Alterman, and viewed this tactic as a blatant misuse and distortion of something beautiful in the service of something ugly and reckless.

If we look, for example, at the first stanza of "Interim Summation" (see page 34), we will note the "full and crammed" night and the "stubborn dull silence" as direct borrowings from the poetic dictionary of Alterman's neo-Symbolism, and yet transplanted to a terrain that is foreign to them in its emotional tone, as well as its linguistic register:

> Yes, the night was full and crammed. At least
> the two of us here, young, at the foot of the bridge.
> Over there benches and low fences.
> Over here a stubborn dull silence breathes.

Avidan, then, operated in a social environment that viewed experimental modernism as ugly, shrill, opaque, and antisocial. The elitist high modernism of T.S. Eliot and Pound was just becoming influential in Israel, and yet Avidan, in his first book, was already saying adieu to Anglo-American modernism. When he writes: "Then behind us / Alfred Prufrock's gloomy love will travel to our towns / across a long and shifting road that will tactfully go round our throats" (see page 36), he relegates Eliot to the archives of modernism as a literary and cultural style that has gone stale. Conversely, it is Tel Aviv and its streets and homes that slowly take off toward a futuristic cosmopolitan urbanity, menacing and enchanting at once. (See "Slowly the Streets Take Off," page 26.)

Years later, upon the publication of the four volumes of Avidan's *Collected Poems****, the poet Aharon Shabtai, in an article for the daily *Yediot Ahronot*, recounts his very first encounter with Avidan. Shabtai was fifteen years old, living and studying in Kibbutz Merhavia:

> "I had finished my three-hour work shift and, sitting in the reading room, I read the scathing review of *Lipless Faucets* in the literary supplement of *Davar* or *Massa*. It was an offensive review, a review that a poet-innovator reaps as a wreath on his head; this is how I first heard of Avidan. At the time, Avidan personified all that was forbidden and deviant. He was the enfant terrible. Today it is impossible to fathom the extent of Avidan's singularity in relation to the self-righteous literary establishment of the time. [...]
>
> "In this context, the circle widens, for this was the moment when Youth began to shake the world. Avidan's book came out more or less around the time when the wave of rock and roll music took hold. Then came the shock of James Dean in *Rebel Without A Cause* (1955), Allen Ginsberg's *Howl and Other Poems* (1956). [...] Youth acquired a heroic aspect: to innovate, to be in constant motion in a world that must renew itself in youth and subversion. This was the essence of Avidan, and it meant having to invent an entirely new Israelism. [...] And therein lay his menace. He championed an Israelism whose horizon was open and daring: open to the erotic, to self-invention, to confrontation, to thinking and debating."

This new Israelism also entailed the creation of a totally new Israeli man—both as a poetic persona and as an actual figure in the poems—as well as a new masculine culture. "Our hands deep in our pockets and warm even in winter. / It is not by chance they've gained young girls' favor"—Avidan writes in "Calling Card" (see page 37), a poem included in his second volume *Personal Problems* (1957). Against the background and culture of the "fighting soldier" (the Palmach, the 1948 war), or a poetry that extols the hardship of the Vagabond or that of the Wandering Jew, Avidan suggests a new model: a carefree city dweller who holds no book or weapon, but keeps his hands nice and warm in his pockets—the source of his erotic and existential vigor.

In 1964 Avidan published *Something for Somebody:Selected Poems 1952-1964*, which comprised a large selection of poems from his four earlier collections, as well as new poems. The early poems underwent minor changes, essentially the combining of two words, which would become one of Avidan's trademarks. In the afterword to the book (titled: "And Something Else"), in his typical serious-droll tone, Avidan explains that this compounding holds a "powerful mystical charge" and allows words to have "a proper social life, unlike people whose fate it is to be solitary." Avidan also produced an album, reciting poems from the book—the first such album in Israel—adopting a deliberate, old-style recitation that served as background and underscored the new "cool" declaiming tone that befits a modern cerebral poet.

During this time his linguistic profile included lexical and syntactical innovations, neologisms, virtuosic and playful usages of the various registers of Hebrew throughout its history, as well as various styles of speech, such as academic, journalistic, and radio-speak. He also introduced colloquial speech in his work and so helped make street language an acceptable part of poetic expression. It can be safely stated that the stylistic and linguistic versatility of Avidan's poetry has no equal in contemporary Hebrew poetry.

Up until *Something for Somebody*, Avidan was focused on building his poetic persona, and his best known and most frequently quoted poems are from this early period—see, for example, "Love Story" (see page 42), "Power of Attorney" (see page 46), "A Sudden Evening" (see page 49), and others. Soon, though, Avidan will try his hand at avant-garde experiments such as concrete poetry, or poems that, for instance, document his responses to a Rorschach test, his experiments with LSD, or his conversations with ELIZA, a computer program written at MIT by Joseph Weizenbaum (*My Electronic Psychiatrist:Eight Authentic Talks with a Computer*, 1974), a text Avidan wrote in English and then translated into Hebrew (see excerpts, page 157).

In a 1963 interview, Avidan described the influence of other poets thus: "I would say that in my earlier poems I was influenced by Russian poetry at the beginning of the [twentieth] century through the work of its Hebrew adherents, an influence that was mostly neutralized by absorbing later Western influences. Still, I don't consider myself a spiritual disciple of any particular poet. The issues that preoccupy me are such that no text by others will help me solve them." And: "During the last fifteen years—which, I believe, constitute my literary evolution—I've been seeking more and more stimulations and simulations, and less and less material proofs. Therefore [...] a science fiction work, of little literary value, may stimulate me in a way that a poem by Eliot cannot. [...] We face the unknown, fervently trying to decode developments and sensations that previous generations of modern authors never thought to consider."

This account of where he stood in 1963 may provide a clue to the kind of poetic work Avidan would undertake in the coming years: no longer a dialogue with literary approaches of recent and distant times, but an attempt to decipher the new rhythms of a changing reality, while acutely aware of cultural transformations (what nowadays we term postmodern and also posthuman). This awareness brought about the overtly obsessive preoccupation of Avidan's work with the very fact of writing poetry, and of being a poet in the second half of the twentieth century, as well as poetry's dramatic relationships (of confrontation, dialogue, and containment) with other genres (prayer, science, logic, lyrics, film, television, and so on).

In this, Avidan diverges from his contemporaries—the poets of "Dor Hamedina"—the generation of Hebrew poets who published their first poems after statehood in 1948. Avidan was never a party to what was conceived of as a shift in poetic norms from the grandiose to the anxious individual seeking to avoid the masses. Avidan's poetry was always grandiose, designed to be read resoundingly in the public square, while also cognizant of the fate of poetry to vanish from the square. Already in the early 1950s, Avidan wrote a wild and hyperbolic ode to a billboard: "No matter that the blush has long been dimmed/upon all the lost faces./I gallop ahead toward you/the advertising billboard,/like a great unprecedented love" ("Billboard," *Lipless Faucets)*. Avidan's work had a different agenda: to remain on the rug of time: "When the rug of time is rolled under our feet/at record speed/it is the acrobats of quality/who manage to hold always and forever/a piece of time under their feet," he says in the poem that concludes the volume *Cryptograms from a Telestar* (1980).

As mentioned, Avidan's greatest fear was staticity and his quest involved constant movement, all the while mindful of the illusion of conquering death through art. And yet, this was an illusion he was willing to entertain:

> but feel a strong urge to flow,
> like a river, alone, in broad daylight,
> to remain always young and to dream
> about a bold rush in broad daylight,
> like a river, alone, to flow, to flow,
> only our body, day by day, grows old.

(Power of Attorney, see page 46)

Or a poem like "Talks" (see page 75) whose repetitive pattern suggests the delaying of the inevitable end, an attempt to create movement in words and so realize, aesthetically, "the simple cutting fact/we have nowhere else to go" ("Power of Attorney"). After twenty-one stanzas, "Talks" ends, declaring itself arbitrary:

> This verbosity will end when this verbosity will end
> And this verbosity will end if this verbosity continues
> And this verbosity will continue when this verbosity
>   will end
>
> Up to here the issue itself and from here other issues
> Up to here other issues and from here the issue itself
> And from here the issue begins and from here the issue
>   is open
> And up to here continuity continues and from here
>   continuity ends

Avidan's last collection *The Latest Gulf: Desert Storm Poems, and Seven Background Poems* (1991) is comprised of two sections: poems in direct and real-time reaction to the first Gulf War, and "background" poems. He published the "reaction" poems in the newspapers, describing their style as "designated writing," namely, a work that has a "definite and immediate publishing objective," as opposed to what he termed "Platonic writing […] that has no external stimulus or deadline."

Indeed, the poems responding to the very first war to be broadcast twenty-four hours a day on TV screens contain no classic elements. The poetry is a dizzying vortex of words, facts, names, assertions, and similes, competing with the militarized and warring reality:

> … words constitute a global power
>> they create situations and void them they move armies
>>> seas continents money corpses other words
>> the world was made in a word and will be unmade in a
>>> word but only he who said Let there be light and there
>>> was light
>> will say Let there be darkness and there was darkness…

("The Latest Gulf," see page 106)

The links Avidan creates between war, poetry, creation, and a poetic avant-garde swiftly drafted, form a composite Avidan made use of throughout his oeuvre, including an intimate and challenging dialogue with Jewish texts and history. In *The Latest Gulf* these stylistic components acquire an old/new expression with a distinct bow to Ezra Pound and his *Cantos*. And the revolutionary modernist (politically conservative) spirit of pre-WWI is also evident in the text. Like Vorticism (so named by Pound in 1913)—the short-lived movement that spawned just two issues of *Blast*—*The Latest Gulf* assumes a combative, uncompromising stance, excepting one aspect: a solemn, nearly fetishist regard for poetry itself, for the poet's freedom of expression and his place in a world of mass communication.

The poem "What Did Kurt Waldheim Expect from the Polish Pope" is among the "background poems" and is the clearest example yet to bear the stamp of Pound's *Cantos* (Avidan translated "Canto

XXXVII" in the late 1970s). In the poem, Avidan says about Pound: "he did for twentieth century's poetry much more than his contemporaries, including Eliot,/his follower, and Auden/and Dylan Thomas and Allen Ginsberg…" This poem, translated into eight languages (including Yiddish, Russian, French, Arabic, and English—the latter by Avidan, see page 151), also appeared in a small volume in 1988, and Avidan, in his hyperbolic fashion, termed it: "super-Canto"; it was the last volume published by the publishing house Avidan had founded and suitably named The Thirtieth Century. In the poem, Avidan cites Hitler: "A nation that doesn't fight once every twenty years is doomed to degeneration," and advises Israeli youths to take this "mindblowing axiom" to heart. Few understood the spirit of the poem and its aesthetic posture, and it was met with a cold, and often disapproving, reception.

We began this short essay with a mention of Avidan's film *Message from the Future* as an example of his attempts to "get off the page and create motion in the real world. We should also note that this film, in fact, is an Israeli version of the Exploitation Film or trash movie in the science fiction genre. "You don't need more than five fingers to control the solar system, or even the galaxy," asserts the messenger from the future in Avidan's film. In the poem of the same title (see page 135) the motives of said messenger are revealed to be:

> nothing but an extremely imaginative Japanese
>   publicity gimmick
> triggering the promo-campaign of mass produced
> electrotelepathors for extensive marketing
> and for popular use. Globally patented.

The vision of a world governed by technological-financial conglomerates, with the blessing and backing of the media and the political establishment, was groundbreaking and futuristic, especially so in Israel of the 1980s, which, as a country with a socialist ethos, had just begun to contend with the sweeping dominance and excesses of capitalism, and, like the rest of the world, was yet to experience the technological revolution. The notion that any concept or value—be it high or low, beautiful or ugly, militant or peace loving—could be appropriated as a commercial and marketing tool, was viewed as alarmist and improbable.

Before *Message* Avidan wrote, produced, and directed four short films, employing a rhythmic and intense montage technique. In one of them, *All Is Possible* (1968), he films himself shooting a pistol exactly on the spot where, three decades later (1995), Prime Minister Yitzhak Rabin would be assassinated at the conclusion of a peace rally. On the soundtrack, the following lines are heard: "The eight conspirators enter the Capitol. Like a band of cats, they approach Cesar from behind."

In addition to filmmaking, Avidan was also an active participant in the visual and conceptual arts in the late 1960s and into the 1970s. He mounted four solo exhibitions, including a show at the Israel Museum, and was part of group shows in Israel and abroad. Following a long visit in the U.S. (see "Improvised Report on the Young Poetry Scene in New York," page 117), Avidan branched out even further: he became an idea- and PR-man; he initiated various projects; he moderated programs for the nascent Israeli television, as well as the radio; he gave poetry workshops (titling them "Executional Perception" and "Creative Fitness") at Tel Aviv University and at Ben-Gurion University of the Negev; he was active in the Labor Party; he was a prolific journalist; and he established numerous non-for-profit organizations, acting as a self-appointed CEO. In Avidan's archives at Ben-Gurion University, there are few drafts of poems but a great number of ideas and proposals for new projects and enterprises, many of them imaginative and innovative.

Avidan tried, by every possible means, to remain relevant and current, to "exist in time" and even overtake and conquer it. Avidan is the poet of longing for the future. A revolutionary shape-shifter throughout his life, he waited for no reader, critic, or fellow artist to catch up with him. He galloped ahead, ever eager for a fresher revolution, even before the ink of the "old" one had dried. It is the essence of this flight forward—both as a recurrent theme in the poet's artistic thought, and as a reflective technique shaping his art—that Avidan's work sought to capture. In "Sadose-manticism," a term he coined, Avidan says, as straightforwardly as one can: "silly to accuse me of sadism/all I'm trying to do is/use words with painful precision/torturing even precision itself" (see page 124). Like every other sadosemantic poetry—like the Dada writers, or Gertrude Stein—Avidan's work invites us to rethink and reexamine language, the language through which we experience ourselves and the world. In his life and work he wished, against all odds, to personify the megaloma-niac ethos of his poetry: to represent the linguistic system itself and to contain all cultural, artistic, and human spheres of the past, present, and those yet to come—all in concert with the po-et's persona, which aims for expansiveness, for the freedom to move in a world where language is made and renewed without the limits of time and space.

In May 1995, at the age of sixty-one, David Avidan was found dead in his apartment in Tel Aviv—alone, ill, and destitute. He did, however, bequeath to us the vital desire to flow toward our preordained future, which, of course, is absolutely unknown.

Anat Weisman
(Translated by Tsipi Keller)

*Comprehensive exams at the conclusion of four years of high school, a prerequisite for higher education in Israel.

**Avidan created new words/rhythms in Hebrew, usually by doing away with hy-phens, and/or combining two words where, for instance, the last letter of the first word is or sounds the same as the first letter of the second word. See footnote 1 on page 28.)

*** Hakibbutz Hameuchad, Bialik Institute, 2009-2011, ed: Anat Weisman and David Weinfeld

DAVID AVIDAN

From *Something for Somebody: Selected Poems 1952–1964* (Schocken, 1964)

Slowly the Streets Take Off

The lovely-lovely street will finally halt in its course.
Tranquility, opaque and hard, will be cut like a challah lengthwise.
And the damp morning will be blackened by a single bolt.
    Its own.

People will breathe heavily as if after an ancient gallop.
The city's cement belt is fastened. Firmly so.
The heavy walls apprehend something and silently fall.

Upon the city dying outside a decisive sunbeam drops.
On such a day it seems no baby is born in the homes,
And no man dies. Indeed, slowly the streets take off.

The streets take off toward the white light like a magic carpet.
The walls that fell are erected somehow (ingenious citizens).
And the city has no beginning and no end. And all entryways
    are blocked.

And your hands sing from the wall like the murmur of greenish
    moss.
And your eyes glow like glass pearls upon the sparkling throat.
Only your weary head floats in the deepening light. And only
    your mouth blows.

The Stain Remained on the Wall

Someone tried to scrub the stain off the wall.
But the stain was too dark (or conversely—too bright).
At any rate—the stain remained on the wall.

So I sent the painter to paint the wall green.
But the stain was too bright.
I hired the plasterer to plaster the wall clean.
But the stain was too dark.
At any rate—the stain remained on the wall.

So I took a kitchen knife and tried to scrape the stain off the wall.
And the knife was awfully sharp.
Only yesterday they sharpened it.
Still.
I fisted an ax and pummeled the wall, but stopped just in time.
I don't know why it suddenly occurred to me
that the wall might fall and still the stain will remain whole.
At any rate—the stain remained on the wall.

And when they put me to the wall, I asked to stand beside it.
And I shielded it with a broad chest (who knows, perhaps).
And when they slashed my back, a lot of blood flowed, but only
     from the back.
They are shooting.
And I truly believed the blood will cover the stain.
A second round of shooting.
And I truly believed the blood will cover the stain.
At any rate—the stain remained on the wall.

Housing

When he was thirty-five
the sporting principle
still guided
his financial life. Perhaps
even excessively so (a big boy
with a bald spot, as
he was once characterized by
some goodgood[1] and veryvery
levelheaded friends). Later—
ten or fifteen or more
years went by with incredible speed. The sons
already at the peak of procreation. The wind
slightly bent his body, and the sun
mercilessly expanded the reign
of the bald spot. Houses damaged
during the battles were repaired. In the meantime,
new ones were built. The wind
would remind him momentmoment that in fact
he was not so young anymore. The sun, too,
as mentioned, was not very generous to him.
And suddenly he wished with all his might
for something of his own. All his days
he was nothing but a hireling, a mere hireling. At least
his own flat, he told himself, at least
a flat that would be entirely his. Another
twenty-five years went by. In the meantime
he paid substantial sums every month

---

1   Avidan created new words/rhythms in Hebrew, usually by doing away with hyphens, and/or combining two words where, for instance, the last letter of the first word is or sounds the same as the first letter of the second word, aiming for cleaner sounds and visuals. He also wished to alleviate somewhat the words' loneliness and endow them with "a proper social life." (Quotes are from Avidan's afterword to *Something for Somebody*.)

toward the flat. And at the end
of said twenty-five years, and he's
about seventy-five, and his wife,
too, by all accounts, is at the edge of the grave,
the flat,
which he had paid for with the best years of his life,
was all his. Now it is possible
to tap the walls with a peace of mind,
stroke the handsome tiles and also feel
you've accomplished something in your life (maybe
simply a legacy, but
the sons already are far away
in time and place). The flat
is like a daughter to you. The bathroom
is all yours, every square foot. And then suddenly
to die
from a difficult illness or from old age or from just
many-many years of fatigue and the used-up
irreparable breaths and distress
with which you've built your home. One
bright day, ancient hands hold on to the hallway walls
as if in a desperate need to apprehend
something solid and durable and permanent
in this sudden fog that has enveloped
you, and which will soon, no doubt,
call upon your spouse.

Longterm Loathing

Ostensibly
you loathe most of the folks
who live with us and with you. All of them
one great foe and not very smart. Even
the best of them—be wary. Still
this is not about some upheaval
resulting from petty contrary interests
and a hostile environment. Frictions
forever nurse on society's primal idiocy,
the primitive anxiety, the narrow-mindedness, hysteria
wasted on trifles. Indeed, you lack
the blessed patience by which
a snowball down the slope is transformed
into so many tubs of cold baths. Instead
of safeguarding an orderly and oh-so-human discretion
on the tiptoes of compulsory harmony, compromises,
and skilled diplomacy that even on the coital bed
drums its digits—slender and bedecked with metal rings—
upon the lace of the sweaty blanket, as if upon
a gilded cigarette case on a table
in one club or another; instead
of being calculated polite and sociable ad-nauseam, you always
assume a militant stance. Somehow
it is often easier even if
in the final account it's a heavy burden,
very-very heavy. Friendship
becomes the peak of human perfections
that move in your sphere. The war—
a worn-out history of gratuitous bombings
that somehow shape the meaning of your wild breaths
in the land of the living; useless battles, perpetually useless,

but put together possibly represent the finest of battles
known to humankind. Individual probity
is the perennial cause of war, and is also
the ammunition and the arms as well as
the final count of losses on the battlefield. Hypocrisy
breathes only the air of conciliation. Possibly,
this is how human civilization was born. The troops
inevitably spawn a different culture. Gradually
you begin to grasp the full meaning
of your place here among the people. The collective
ventures, the heritage of generations, the humanism
that is the goodhearted father of allofus, are mostly
devoid of identity and character. Enmities
form the rare summits of your poetry. Afflictions
are the rarefied air blowing across remote altitudes. The snow,
except for very few and distinct instances, remains
always-always frozen unloving and cold, always
frozen unloved and hardly breathing, but
always-always very close to the sky. The sun
is a warm bright gigantic illusion which has,
among other things, a physical life. The exact
sciences always know how to voice
a few words of wisdom on the subject. But
this is not the key. The snowy heights
are the sun's unvanquished rivals, they laugh
at her[2] from within the white death. Somehow
they're often the sun's only friends. At least the sun
is certainly beautiful, certainly beautiful. Within
a system of very materialistic principles you realize that animosity
grows firstofall due to overcrowding, lethargy, and the limitations
of creatures with no vision no kindness existing
in an atmosphere of extremely compressed air where

---

2   In Hebrew, sun is a feminine noun.

they also crush the great snows with their feet
and will never understand the sun. In the vast
sweeps of spiritual freedom where perhaps
one day you'll be fortunate to walk alone, as if
at the funeral of the human race and yet without
even one solitary human witness, you may learn
to squeeze from yourself a smile of benign compassion
and take to heart the ancient pains of the land of slavery
        you've escaped,
the repulsive infantilism of matter forever howling
like a famished infant in a filthy crib, or like
a blind kitten on wet sand, or like any other kind
of newborn. Only there—
in the vast sweeps of this freedom,
of this escape, of this very longterm loathing,
to die—
namely, to perceive during the short moment of death
the entire beautiful earth beneath you. The valleys,
after all, are really only part of the full picture. Naturally,
a myriad of pitfalls, but on the whole the earth
is beautiful and wide and loved, at least
when you observe it from above, as the light
freezes in the eye allatonce like some wondrous diamond
from childhood dreams or fairytales about dwarves,
while dying is the definite circumstance of your short
        biography, and the gaze
is clear and sober and last. And then in vain
your dead hands suddenly shoot up
in a mad hope to go back, go back down below,
go back and yield. After all,
the lofty proud snow
won't let go of its old friends. Death
patiently wraps you and sets you rolling

in any random direction. The sun
surveys the plane of the white heights
with a nearly resigned look, as if
once again she has endured a small defeat,
a very small defeat, although
the victory is a great one indeed.

Interim Summation

Yes, the night was full and crammed. At least
the two of us here, young, at the foot of the bridge.
Over there benches and low fences.
Over here a stubborn dull silence breathes.

Yes, the night is full and crammed. At least
they didn't hang us from low fences.

And we tried to see this night
with benevolent eyes. We even tried
here and there to express principled beliefs
and presumably we did.

Yes, the night was stark and honest
and I was more or less contented.

Later she zipped herself up with a zipper
and suddenly we stood and started walking.
And we saw how a warm wind covers over
darkness and a cement floor. Filthy.
And the bridge seemed like some ruined city
we had left behind and went walking.

At any rate—it was a typical night out
(embellishing charged to aging).

And yet why did we feel so distinctly
that we came back as if to a *different* land
that is all benches and density of walls
the streets swept clean and the hour late.

As said, it was a typical night out
(misgivings to be charged to aging).

When we got home it was almost morning.
We went up. We yawned. We made coffee.
And the built city panted toward morning
like a woman in heat toward a handsome male.
And the built city groaned toward morning
like a throat to a knife. And morning fell
like a cool white parachute. And the morning
a clear summermorning even fair.

At any rate—it was a typical summer morning
(exaggerations to be charged to aging).

Concerning the Gloomy Love of J. Alfred Prufrock

One day the sober wisdoms will come to wake us
from our dull and heavy slumber, like cannonballs
on a very bright Saturday morn. Then behind us
the gloomy love of Alfred Prufrock will travel to our towns
across a long and shifting road that will tactfully go round our
    throats—
and there it will become when the time comes
a well-preserved collection of late recollections
yet our poems will refuse to take and be taken
and this will be a sure sign of our youthful ways.

And yet either way every resistance breaks.
Let us then take the last road
leading to our seashore, to the sands,
into the kingdom of lost precincts where only
we are allowed entry, and the secret password
is to be delivered firmly but softly,
and there is a door that will open and shut,
and there is always yet another untried
way, and the day is still wide open and long.

And there, in underwater housing projects, sea-girls
will float across our knees, a look of frightened bliss
on their faces as well as the memory of skies
too high and too many eyes
and the incessant question who's coming who's coming,
and there, to the distant sound
of a musical interlude, we will spread
our legs and suck their lips until we drown.

Calling Card

We go in the night, go go go
along the long and filthy roads.
Days of peace. No rifle in the weeds.

But the going never comes to an end
even though we've said our goodbyes to one and all
and the last debt was finally paid off.

Whence have we come where are we going and no end in sight?
Are we quite certain we've had time to love?
And why have we been so betrayed by the good end?

With ease we carry our young bodies.
It is not a world of indifference that led us to a world of frivolities.
The final report on us is drawn from erroneous sources.

We'll respond to all questions in a very definite order.
Our hands deep in our pockets and warm even in winter.
It is not by chance they've gained young girls' favor.

It is not by chance we swiftly crossed worlds.
It is not by chance long nomadic roads are so uniform.
It is not by chance we missed all the forewords.

Dance Music

We reflected at length. Light flooded
the forehead's rectangle, the eyes, the eyebrows. We asked
the same questions and were answered
as always. Winter arrived
and saddened us. From others
we asked nothing and from ourselves
we asked only little. But we knew
that daylight is not hostile and that night
is only a passing nuisance. Rain came
and silenced the tune. We turned on the radio,
dimmed the lights, and quietly dove
into dark and shadowy depths. The hairy creature
awoke in us. Man alone is the aim
of all creation. And so
woman found us. We were
hard and festive until nightfall.
Why did light flood the eyes, eyebrows,
the forehead's rectangle, the back, the body. The rain,
why did it come, and how to explain
that we went under and did not sink.

Preamble

From all the faraway places the voice will come,
like the voice of the drum, indistinct, rhythmic. Our ears
will be listening as if to a great orator
who has suddenly risen before us.
And then the laughter will come, brief, croaky,
like a creaking engine. Our minds
will open to it as if to a hymn to liberty,
ringing high above us.
Later will come the commentary,
loving but also invalidating
all the universes my ardor has erected,
and, in the end, it too will disintegrate.

Process

The white water asked for an extension
to turn darker. And then
an unfamiliar ripple ran across the surface
and allatonce something was perverted
but still remained within the bounds
of perversions that are always tolerated,
perversions that bespeak flaws and gradations
and also an abiding artful truth.

Sedation

Even then he felt thoroughly refreshed,
a youthful figure and a greedy snout,
and the sudden delight that descended on him like a cloud.
And then he felt that his strength had returned
and that everything was so very silly,
and suddenly a feeling of ecstasy,
and suddenly a crazy desire to open up
fully fully to the appalling delight.
To open up, without holding back, like a sleeping bag
in which all the seams have been unraveled down to the last
toward the absolute night, leaving not
even one tiny thread of individuality.
And to desist desist desist
and to be complete complete complete.
And to be swept up by the great cascade
and to be picked up by the great wind
and yet, without losing the taste
for the sudden feeling of bliss.
Remember always: You're in bed with a woman
and not with some cosmic harmony.
And so they stitch you up like a sleeping bag
within minutes of your suicide.
And so they rob you of the joy,
and so they rob you of your death,
and so they spare you the folly.

Love Story

Oh how I knew to die for you and how
I knew not to live for you.

And they told me long ago, how beautiful, and where you're from,
that you loved me once verymuch, and still do.
They also told me some time ago that your name, I believe,
    is Ruchama,
and, by the way, it fits you well, I mean your dress.
You know, many rumors arrive from there,
and in fact I've been waiting for you to arrive today.
Oh how I knew to die for you and how
I knew not to live for you.

And my days in perfect silence whispered to you unbroken
    whispers
with each incidental wind that caressed your bare breasts.
And with each caress you sighed it's evening already.
Of course, you were mistaken. It was morning, but a sad morning.
And one day you suddenly felt you're of age already
and the wind went drifting among the reeds.

And the water in the lake was deep. And when darkness
glided across like a dinghy, a formless
apprehension in the chest cavity caused pain. And when darkness
did not glide across like a dinghy, silence
squeezed your body like a giant python. But darkness
was not the problem. And when the morning sun loomed

you understood that night had gone and you went away from there,
tried and worried more than ever before.
And I asked you seriously how are you Ruchama

and how did you injure your hand.
And you smiled and said ah it's from over there.
Oh, if only you could understand, but you never could,
never understood how I knew to die for you and how
I knew not to live for you.

Of course you'll end up going back there one day,
and I will see you part of the way and then turn back.
And I doubt I'll turn my head to look at you. Oh, how
some incidental wind will brush my bare chest.
And after a while I'll try to guess if you got there already,
and then I'll forget anew every sad morning.
And if in moments of weakness I'll remember you Ruchama,
dark reeds will protect you.

And if in a powerful moment of weakness I'll desire you
and hurriedly walk toward the lake
an incidental wind will surely come running and whistle in you,
and you'll undress, there'll be a rustle in the lake,
but I'll find your clothes only. Then perhaps an old
hopeless love will rasp in you. In the lake a lost
stillness will anchor with a whisper. And an incidental
wind will flutter there and then will go silent in you.

A Short Outing that Ended Well

Well, hello,
hello to manly handshakes, hello
to handshakes and friendship and hello
to the presumed love. For many days
dinghies made their way toward the hazardous estuary,
many-many days have since gone past and the dinghies
are still on their way to the hazardous estuary
in the wet sunlight. The sails
have been meticulously folded and packed
in paper bundles. In the dense breeze
the pipes have been driven between the jaws, and the tobacco
pouches untied. A match
was cautiously but assuredly struck. There was
a lot of smoke and thoughts of smoke and thoughts.
We were all so pumped up for trouble, so at peace
with the inevitable danger of the estuary, and so
merry and solemn (only the feet
leapt onto the bank in time). Well, hello,
hello to the wind blowing as usual
between me and the familiar objects, between
me and the forbidden thoughts and also
between me and the ancient friendship. Let us
go down the old stone steps, leading
to all the dusty memories of childhood, to all
the sweet and drowsy oblivions, to all
the peaks where the wind has never blown
and probably never will, and there
we will sprint round-round with the world's fastest turtles,
we will kick with the tips of our shoes the heap of gravel in the fields
and climb the trees that haven't grown or shrunk, and we will
    watch—

oh how we will watch and watch. But tomorrow,
in the thin cool morning, between me
and the wind forever blowing between me
and the faraway salvation, a sudden distant
sound of falling stones, a distant sound
of stones upon some road, and anyhow,
we will still believe there is something to fight for,
and that the old truths still hold, that there is
enough room for love in our brains, that there are
worse places thanthis in the world. And so
we will go back down the old stone steps
to the clear and horny air
of the urban plane where we will live
and die.

Power of Attorney

(for whom it may concern)

What justifies most of all
the loneliness, the great despair,
the peculiar submission to the burden
of the great loneliness, the great despair,
is the simple cutting fact
we have nowhere else to go.

On clear nights the air is cold
and at times on cloudy nights as well,
and there's rain and heat waves
and beautiful bodies and also faces
that sometimes smile and sometimes don't,
sometimes because of him, sometimes because of her.

The landscape is simple and unambiguous,
angels do not climb up or down the ladder,[3]
sometimes we hate, sometimes we love,
we have a few friends, and mostly foes,
but feel a strong urge to flow,
like a river, alone, in broad daylight,
to remain always young and to dream
about a bold rush in broad daylight,
like a river, alone, to flow, to flow,
only our body, day by day, grows old.

What justifies most of all
the dream, the great despair,
the knowledge that there is no justification

---

3   Alludes to Jacob's Ladder, Genesis 28:10-19.

and looking for it anew every moment,
the excitement, the dread,
what justifies most of all,
what justifies the great despair
is the simple cutting fact
we have nowhere else to go.

Only our body, day by day, grows old,
and we a river in broad daylight
alone to flow, to flow alone,
what justifies, what justifies the dream,
what justifies the great despair,
what justifies most of all.

P.S. The nights are clear and the air is cold,
there's fervor and drive but no love,
and already no smile and already no words,
angels do not climb up or down the ladder,
the poems, as is their way, only tell
what can be told in words,
and so off a cliff they pitch themselves
down to the great sea where waves
rise and fall, rise and fall.

Personal Problems

Because I loved you so much I couldn't tell you.
I couldn't tell you I loved you so much.
I loved you so much.
Until other days came and I could tell you.
I could tell you because I loved you.
Because I loved you.
The trees blossomed in green and the sun grew dark.
And the more I loved you the darker it grew.
Distant. Ready to pounce. Like a certain breed of panther.
(Truly, it did remind one of a panther.)
And then we came to town.
A lily knew me.
In the morning she woke me.
And still I loved you.
Final light came and swept aside all doubt
and only the movie house remained behind,
white and blazing in the sun.
He who has something to hide
must not be seen in daylight.
And he who loves must not go into town.

A Sudden Evening

An old man—what is his life?
He rises in the morning, and a morning does not rise in him.
He shuffles to the kitchen where
tepid water will remind him that at his age,
at his age, at his age,
an old man—what are his mornings?
He rises on a summer day and already autumn
blends in the evening with the lightbulb in his room.
He has yet to return from his trip to the hallway
where he pondered, pondered, pondered
what to do now and what to read,
an old man—what are his books?
Strong winds will leaf through them,
marking phrases about the end of time
in invisible ink, and then a few
will be revealed to him. And he will revolt,
with a flare in his eye, against his vast experience,
an old man—what are his eyes?
If he concentrates, the memory of a long-ago
battle will surface, a thirst for conflicts and skills
and steep odds, until the day of stupor is near.
Now up his throat, like scouts,
some of his most confident grunts cautiously rise,
like the growl of a young tiger in autumn,
an old man—where are all his tigers?
He may yet set out on a hunt some day
when the green will turn blackgreen,
with great vigor and little practice
he may yet set out on a hunt some day.
He will leave the years behind him
like a long road, worn out and left behind

a wild car that he himself will drive, as if
chasing time that has already been spent,
an old man—what does he have at his age?
Afraid to fall asleep he drowses,
his half-shut eyes follow the movement
of stars, evaluate whether the murmurs intimate
that this is his last night,
an old man—what does he have in the window?
An open window beyond which an alien
indistinct head signals that he must again
become a young tiger in autumn, he must
always always take, never let
a hostile head beyond the window
come calling on the last evening
an old man—what is his evening?
Not a king
he will fall
not on his sword.

Missed Opportunity

Alone out into the night? Alone
out into this wet night? Alone
out into this fading night? To the nearby square
you[4] will take a hundred lonely steps. Then
I will join you of my own ill will, no headlights,
no horn, no good
intentions, no
signals.
Nourished by jittery rains in this brightened forest,
just eight traffic lights grow, shedding
toward spring ripe police helmets,
sheltering transparent and deadly morning birds,
dictating the pace of locomotion. You're a cat,
you're a kitten, you're a small wet sorceress, riding vacuum cleaners
up to tall windows, mixing sweet and popular poison under
    colorful awnings,
murmuring charming snubs in a hushed engine-tongue, recalling
the day of reckoning.
I could, of course, bring you to me, dry you off
near the electric heater, dry you off
with my bodyheat, grant you
incremental bliss calculated down to the last detail
until morning, the unavoidable morning, until the rise
of the confident efficient sun that peels
men's heads off their cosseted youth. The hair
that one day disappears from men's heads drifts,
as if accidentally, to women, like a tease, like a warning
of what's to come to those who come. The women rebuff the hair
with whispers and invocations they've learned not from their
    grandmas,

---

4   The addressee is female.

nonetheless, it scratches our young shoulders, crying out, demanding
    demanding
the right to self-determination, recounting the birthdays, the
    exigency
of transformation.
It is time to admit that a place is needed, needed urgently,
a cozy and rational place where one can shout,
a place where one can vent and weep in, a place
is needed. Meanwhile,
we're already clad in the new toga, shod
in light Roman sandals, armed with heavy spears,
breathlessly awaiting the blinding light, the clear drone
of a flying saucer, the sharp pain of the alien touch
in our strained brain centers. Alone
out to the morning? Alone
out to this dry morning? Alone
out to this fateful morning? Before evening
I will take a thousand friendly steps. Then
you will join me of your own good will, high beams on,
horns honking, outfitted with decidedly
lewd intentions and with all
the toofamiliar signals I'll no longer
know how to read.

Experiments in Hysterics

There are people who've got nothing to lose, there are people
who've got nothing. What
haven't they got, what
haven't they got to lose? There are people
who've got a time bomb inside, they've got
time inside that will soon explode. What
have they got inside that will soon, what
have they got to lose? And there are, of course,
other ways to formulate the feeling. It's possible, for instance,
to decelerate atonce the wheel of reflexes, then suddenly
everything regains its crystalline form. They're visible,
those who've got nothing to lose, they're visible, you see them,
you may even see them in the form of an advanced submarine,
a submarine in fact that hasn't been tested yet, a submarine in fact
that may never be tested. The deep waters
receive it with a quivering sigh. This is
their big moment. They have no
qualms about the speed, they have no
other speed to offer. Yet it is clear
that this is not the point, the point is this:
Will the walls hold up or not? Of course,
of course they will. The fortune tellers, the best among them,
have nodoubt, they have concerns, yes, but the best, the very
best among them have nodoubt. And so this is the point:
Will they or will they not hold up? And the more important
        question—
and there's noneed, although the possibility exists, possibility
        always exists,
to couch it in powerfully rousing similes—the more important
question, the most important, is this: Am I—and suddenly for
        some reason

in first person, leaving noroom for mistakes—am I
already afraid or still afraid, already
afraid or still already
afraid?
Very important, then, to keep writing. One must not
miss opportunities. Immortalize yourself while
there's still time, before you tumble. Tomorrow you'll be changed,
    tomorrow
will be late. Tomorrow
is always late. This is
the system, there's no other. There is a later one, but
it will be implemented, certainly implemented, only tomorrow, only
when it will be too late. Come, come with me. Summer
will never return. The earth
begins to travel. Tomorrow
I'll take you to the circus. Everything
will travel in the circus. To the sound of a distant chime
the crust of the earth will move slowly-slowly, with an
    overwhelming effort
and full accountability. There will never be
a more accountable movement. Come, come
to the sudden joy, remember me fondly, speak
of me fondly on that other morning when I'll awake anew
into the murderous unreal speed of impressions
to which I am enslaved, it seems, irrevocably.

Summer 1962

(draft for a cool screenplay)

A man waves hello to a woman.
A woman waves hello to a man.
Half the world waves hello
to its other half.
A fleeting alert moment, nearly imperceptible,
as everything moves, settling into two parallel rows,
waiting. The sun crosses in the middle, as if through a formation,
not turning left or right, not granting either of the rows
any glow-attention, a grade, or a promotion,
but spins on with dubious speed, howling
like a red boar pierced with African spears,
and yet tarries to depart.
A moment of confusion. What will come
of it? Will something come of it? Will someone
come out of it?
The initiative, well hidden in the facial folds, refuses
to enlist, reveals
treacherous pacifist tendencies, and only at the finish
submissively begins to reassess. An expression of "Yes, but,"
on the aloof face. Yes but, yes but, yes but. But,
is this for me? Is this for you?
Could you compete with my self-love?
Could you compete with your self-love?
Could we compete? A moment of clarity,
a moment of risk. The snazzy killer
sharpens a photogenic razor on his victim's tie.
With surprising grace he defies the inevitable
noose that has been lurking since his early youth.
He entertains. Reaps applause. American humor.

He drips promptly, heatedly, heavily, like tropical rain,
over the distant sounds of the church's choir, attempts
to turn to mist before reaching the ground, but seeps
into it with a desperate wail. And now is the time
to go back and recall, for a fleeting alert moment, nearly
     imperceptible,
go back and recall for a moment the nebulous rules of engagement.
The practiced fingers on the typewriter are a marvelous fountain
of kinetic energy. They possess all the necessary means
to destroy the world. The world possesses all the necessary
means to be destroyed by them, to die with a kiss. At last,
we've come to the kiss, to the longed-for assent. Ambiance
is a charming camouflage netting, calmly spread over open hazards.
It demands frequent victims, and not only in the framework of art.
It curbs the dear end, in order to become once and for all time,
     once and not for all time,
something else, to become something more than it is. And now is
     the time
to go back and forget anew, once and not for alltime, the rules
of engagement. We've lived through
yet another winter. We live
between summer and summer. The intricate delusion
of the gradual progression between the seasons
is our best defense. After all,
where else in the world
does such a wonderful sun still remain, as it does
in the Mediterranean Basin? Not to mention
that we came here on the strength of an ancient edict
that no one can contest or rival. We file it anew
every summer as it summers, every summer as it ends.[5]

---

5   In the Hebrew: "ka'itz b'keitzo kaitz b'kitzo"— "ka'itz b'keitzo" alludes to the rabbinical
construction that denotes routine, repetition; "ka'itz b'kitzo"—a play on "kai'tz" (summer) and
"ketz" (end).

And there's water, sun and water, water and sun, water and water.
    In the beginning
there was water, and the spirit of God moved upon the face of
    the water.[6]
In the end there will be water, and the spirit of God will move upon
the face of the water. And while there's in the world more water
than nowater, more sun than nosun, it is permissible still
to plan quietly and with relative ease for the next
generation. Now
something must move from here to there, must set
in motion the inevitable exit without which
there is no art and no renewal. With this in mind,
the stranger walks farther away, deep into the long
and never-ending boulevard. A man
waves hello to a woman. A woman
waves hello to a man. Half the world
departs allatonce from its other half. Most importantly:
the red boar, pierced with African spears,
has recovered with surprising speed
and returned to his rightful place. Odd:
he's done it again.

---

6   Genesis 1,2.

Moment before Last

The body pleaded with the spirit: Stay
here. You'll see, it'll be
fun. Today, at long last, I'll open
all the old wine bottles.
Even the circus will come here.
I'll sing you songs you haven't heard before.
But the spirit said: What's the matter with you?
Have you forgotten already that my pleasure
is motion in time? Now
I'm getting out of here. Are you
coming with me ornot?

Kas Buvo – Tai Nebus[7]

Two Lithuanians, who remember their mother tongue
even less than they remember
their mothers, meet on a cool evening
in a café and reminisce.
How do you say past in Lithuanian?
Really, how do you say
past in Lithuanian? Very embarrassing, really
very embarrassing. Maybe there is someone
in this pleasant neighborhood, within a radius
of a kilometer or two, who can fix
this daunting linguistic short circuit?
But already the hour is very late
and all the Lithuanians stillliving
are already sleeping.

How do you say sleep in Lithuanian?

---

7   Lithuanian: "What was, won't be."

Morning and Evening March

The sophisticated mirrors, the art of photography,
the film industry, and every other innovation
in these or other fields, allow you, more than your predecessors,
to view yourself from the outside. The evolution of the street
and the resulting evolution of streetlanguage allow you—
again, more than your predecessors—to fearlessly blend
in your most intimate and un-addressable[8] prayers
phrases such as: "Let yourself go."
Well, then, let, let yourself go—just be careful
not to lose, not even for an instant, your bold image,
the whoosh of its back as it gets away from you always and forever,
and the awful invitation to never let yourself rest. Let yourself
follow it close behind, morning and evening, midnight
and noon. Keep up
the pace, so you don't stumble and get lost
in the snow, should there be snow, and in the desert,
should there be a desert.

---

[8] The Hebrew "hassar-ma'an" also evokes "unanswered."

A Peek into an Open Dream

1. Psychotherapy

The seven skinny cows[9]
said to the Nile, on behalf
of the forest: Die,
die, die child. You'd be
better off. Tomorrow you'll find
fine gold fluttering in the wind
among the dreadful reeds.

2. Resisting Therapy

The seven fat cows
said to the forest, on behalf
of the Nile: Grow,
grow, grow, death. You
must. Tomorrow a pale fire
will come out of the bush[10]
and initiate contact with you.

3. The Prescription

The seven skinny cows
said to the seven fat cows: Enough
for now. Both the Nile and the forest
are ready for a truce. Now
at last we'll begin to settle

---

9   Alludes to Pharaoh's dream, Genesis 41, 1.
10   Alludes to Moses' vision of the burning bush, Exodus 3,2.

the ancient issues between us.
Dream number one,
over.

4. The Peeping Tom's Comment

And this too is possible: The seven
fat cows asked the seven skinny cows:
Now, frankly, how do you manage
to maintain such a great figure?

FUTUREMAN

DAVID AVIDAN

From *Practical Poems*
(The Thirtieth Century,
Levin–Epstein Modan, 1973)

Those Who Do Not Know How to Ask

In August 1966, when I returned after
a year abroad, I was often asked
if I had returned for good—a typical
Israeli question. Well, no,
no, thanks, really, no, I didn't come back
to die in the Holy Land, if this is
what you meant. Many thanks for
your benevolence. My compliments.
Please come always. My compliments.
Come, go, come, go.

Six Local Poems

1. before man

Before man goes to bed man takes off
his pants and hangs them on a chair
arranges for a wake-up call and goes to the throne
from hereon bathroom from hereon
restroom from hereon the john
before man goes to bed man takes off his clothes
checks himself in the mirror and goes
to bed with the worry flicker in the center
of an astronaut's eyeball
with guidance on how to improve landing
how to improve speech
when one lands and goes to sleep

2. man hangs

Man hangs his pants and plans his manhood
hangs his pants on a chair and takes a stance
takes a stance regarding his future poems and brings down a leg
brings down a leg casts a glance in the mirror and makes a movie
makes a movie hangs his pants and makes plans
takes a stance regarding his future plans and brings down
brings up looks in the mirror and makes a movie
man puts on his pants and presides over his reign
such and such a distance from the goods to his fly
up to here his debts and from here his returns
man wears out his pants and spreads his land
to the east and west north south[11] and to anyplace
the Sixth Fleet and the Red Fleet may reach

---

11   Alludes to Genesis 28,14: "And thou shalt spread abroad to the west, and to the east, and
to the north, and to the south." The verse is also a popular folk song.

3. when man rises

When man rises in the morning man puts on
his pants and instantly opens fire upon
his bed his balcony his books
upon the jets of water in hot pursuit
of him a drowsy man rises in the morning
unafraid to put on his pants and open fire

4. man pesters

Man returns to his flat and pesters a machine
pesters a typewriter out of season
man pesters a typewriter and delays his sleep
how many minutes hours years will he remain awake
man awakes his typewriter and pesters his sleep
man returns to his flat and turns on a machine
more or less the right machine
man turns on a wake-machine and delays his sleep
for how many minutes hours years will he remain awake
in this flat in this land and in anyplace
the Sixth Fleet and the Red Fleet may reach

5. summing up

before man
man hangs
when man rises
man pesters

6. tax-free supplement for diplomatic relations expenditure

Two words on the problematic status of erections
against the backdrop of the waning class warfare

and the hardening positions of the superpowers:
it is clear, for instance, that each visible hardening
is more and more visible vis à vis a softening, a slight softening,
and a sizeable softening of the other side which, by the by,
is only rarely soft enough to allow a real hard position
to bloom fully in secure and agreed-upon borders
with minimum speech-letting
and God the Lord will take pity on all Jews
and Allah on all Muslims
and the armies of GodtheLordIsraelandGodtheLordAllah
will clear away words and dung
day and night.
This is the framework
voted verified certified
for a peace-strike
to be initiated
when the time comes
right after the war.

Long Term and Short Term

"But it will pay off in the long term"—
hogwash.
Nothing will pay off in the longterm
because longterm
never pays off.
First, it is not long
so what's the use discussing length.
Second, it is not a term
for it has nothing to do with terming.
Third, it doesn't pay off
because purchasing power decreases with age:
Fact.
Therefore, short term it doesn't pay off
to talk about longtermplans.
Short term it pays off to wed a woman
give her five kids
and leave.

Violation Ticket to the Messiah for Weeping in Public

Don't weep, whipped child—
the entire world awaits you
and you await the entire world,
trying meanwhile to raise[12] everyone.
All day long you diligently seek
whom to raise and where
and come evening you release
upon a depleted locale
a wretched discharge[13]
a fire hydrant

Penalty Notice:

messiah messiah
you're a mess
a romantic child
a troubled orphan
a wretched discharge
a fire hydrant
your father is not a man
your mother is not pretty
you were born here
and here you will die
messiah pariah
a hopeless case

---

12   In slang usage also means: to lay, to make out with.
13   In Hebrew: "shficha harufa"—a pun on "shifcha harufa," a wretched maid,
see Leviticus 19, 20. See also Babylonian Talmud Tractate 33a.

Filing

Short or long—sort out
prolonged indecision—elaborate
girls
job offers
plenty deficit—maneuver credit
Tel Aviv nightlife
(marriage at times is a pleasant enough business)
celebratory masturbation
with recurring data
regimented despair and once in a while
personal freedom in late morning
an erect member
and a disconnected telephone

Liquidation Sale

So this is the end of the story from here it's only
possible to begin anew a black poodle
impregnates his niece with the blessing of her owner
at the red light near the car tires
a quiet night no police cruisers no bank
will be robbed until morning a stable peace
only the old jaws chomp all night
on the retreating flesh
the palate the tongue and the lips
the root of the nose
so this is the end of the story beauty has gone
and what's left are the black jaws
of a black poodle impregnating in early evening
a couple of snow tires with controlled passion
all the barking all the honking and the feet stomping
lead to Rome but begin in Jerusalem

Insignificant Deviation from the Socio-Genetic Code of the Average Family Cell

This is all I need
kids that will suddenly appear
in this desolation
they may even fertilize it
for a few years
but then I will never emerge
from under

Outside the desert of marriage
there's nothing
but this nothing
is all a man is allowed to hope for
in this wasteland
where he waits
wherein and from where he practices freeplay
of not in and not out
and with mounting anxiety anticipates
the ever-shrinking odds

Meantime he tells himself
not to rise and not to raise
not to build and not to be rebuilt[14]
not to sit and not to leave

and not to keep
his word

---

14 Alludes to the 1930s folk song: "We came to the land to build and to be rebuilt in it."

Talks

You talked to me about love I talked to you about money
I talked to you about money you talked to me about trust
I talked to you about trust you talked to me about a child
I talked to you about a child you talked to me about love
I talked to you about love you talked to me about sex
I talked to you about sex you talked to me about acclaim

I talked to you about acclaim you talked to me about your mother
I talked to you about literature you talked to me about your girlhood
I talked to you about my childhood you talked to me about a child
I talked to you about a child you talked to me about trust
I talked to you about trust you talked to me about sex

I talked to you about sex you talked to me about movies
I talked to you about movies you talked to me about overseas
I talked to you about overseas you talked to me about your grandpa
I talked to you about my grandpa you talked to me about your
    grandma

I talked to you about me you talked to me about music
I talked to you about music you talked to me about art
I talked to you about art you talked to me about fashion
I talked to you about fashion you talked to me about movies
I talked to you about movies you talked to me about a child

I talked to you about pregnancy you talked to me about the pill
I talked to you about the pill you talked to me about sex
I talked to you about sex you talked to me about beauty
I talked to you about beauty you talked to me about cosmetics

I talked to you about cosmetics you talked to me about you
I talked to you about you you talked to me with difficulty
You talked to me with difficulty I talked to you with ease
I talked to you with ease you talked to me calmly

I talked to you calmly you took a shower
I took a shower you put on a record
I read the newspaper you solved a crossword puzzle
I went up to the apartment above you went to the apartment next door
I rang the bell of the apartment next door and went downstairs

I got the mail and went up to the apartment above
I buzzed you on the phone you buzzed me back
I got the operator and dialed myself
You buzzed me on the phone I buzzed you back

I talked to myself about you you talked to yourself about me
I talked to myself about tomorrow you talked to yourself about
    yesterday
I talked to myself about New York you talked to yourself about
    Frankfurt

I waited for myself minutes you waited for yourself years
I waited for myself years you waited for yourself a month
I waited for myself a month you waited for yourself an evening
I waited for myself an evening you waited for yourself a night

And now I sum up and you don't sum up
And now you do sum up and I don't sum up
And now I add and now you subtract
And now I subtract and now you don't add

Look for me today and I'll look for you tomorrow
Look for me tomorrow and I'll look for you the day after
I looked for you yesterday because you looked for me the day before

Meantime I'll get going meantime you won't get going
Meantime you'll get going meantime I'll come back
Meantime you'll come back meantime I'm going out
Meantime I come back meantime you stay put

I talked to you about talking you talked to me about facts
I talked to you about facts you talked to me about explication
I talked to you about explication you talked to me about love

I talked to you about love you talked to me about summer
I talked to you about summer you talked to me about time
I talked to you about time you talked to me all the time
I talked to you all the time you talked to me about tonight
I talked to you about tonight and you went to the apartment next door

And now I disconnect and now you too disconnect
And now I connect and now you too connect
Wait on the road at midnight and I'll arrive exactly at midnight
Wait on the road at ten and I'll arrive exactly at ten
Buy tickets to the movies and we'll go to the movies
If there's a matinée we'll go to a matinée

And now it's final till tomorrow till tonight till morning
And now it's final with me and now it's final with you
I talked to you about the end you talked to me about you
I talked to you about me you talked to me about a child

I talked to you about love you talked to me about money
You talked to me about money I talked to you about trust
You talked to me about trust I talked to you about a child
You talked to me about a child I talked to you about privacy
You talked to me about love I talked to you about privacy
You talked to me about privacy I talked to you about sex

We waited for ourselves minutes we waited for ourselves years
And now we subtract and now we add
Meantime we go out meantime we come back
We looked for ourselves today we'll look for ourselves tomorrow

This verbosity will end when this verbosity will end
And this verbosity will end if this verbosity continues
And this verbosity will continue when this verbosity will end

Up to here the issue itself and from here other issues
Up to here other issues and from here the issue itself
And from here the issue begins and from here the issue is open
And up to here continuity continues and from here continuity ends

What I[15] Have to Say to You, Until Next Time

I love the quiet you leave behind you
I love the death emanating from your poems
I love the quick pace of your films
I love the noise that precedes you

I love the quiet you leave behind you
I love the grass you trample under your feet
I love the idea of death and your life insurance
and I love your name and all your assets

I love the quiet you leave behind you
I love the room when empty of you
I love the water that swells up above you
I love the darkness that undermines you

I love the quiet you leave behind you
I love the sound crawling at your feet
I love the moment when I'm left without you
I love the distant color of your eyes

I love the quiet you leave behind you
and I sit here quietly and think about you
how large you were and scary in the flesh
and how I will now manage here without you

I'm afraid of the quiet you leave behind you
and I sit and think how it will be without you
and I recall those who came before you
and I sit here quietly and think of you

---

15   The speaker is female.

Four Flashes

1. Oral Law

Men change
women
and God changes
men
but no one changes God
therefore the aforementioned is constant

2. Farewell Note

Your sweet memory
in my body
your manhood deep
in my mouth
thanks for everything
it was nice
come over sometime
we'll have coffee

3. Check-Out Before Noon

Sunshine
at the window
yesterday
at the hotel
all was real
exact and impersonal
and now the entire episode
is nauseating

4. Morning Indulgences

A woman in bed
goes up in smoke
an electric tan
a first-rate plum
a baked apple
compulsive preening
one must not gain weight
think of sex
think of money
think of garments
all men
are bastards and cheaters

Burying Uncle Solomon

Fresh color in the cheeks wings and strong winds
no god in the sky fish in the water birds in a tree
a back on a bed a bed on a floor an apartment building
a cold flag diligent people dug-up earth
and now two three deep breaths and a sneeze
a messiah is born in a sneeze in the baying of a donkey
in a wag of a tail in a door slamming in a hoe's blow
a messiah is born in the maternity ward of Hakirya

No talking quietly in twos threes sixes
wrapped in gauze a stretcher bearer in front and one in back
a messiah is born in the maternity ward in Jaffa
and Uncle Solomon is buried on a hot day in Holon[16]
align the tires align the steering wheel bumper-to-bumper
license plate to green green to license plate a slope in the sand

Mordechai's son? Mordechai's son. And his wife and daughters
his sister her family old acquaintances did you know him
the deceased never thought about the end he liked to smoke
birds and flies nested in his head and a poisonous snake
sat between his lungs and waited for a signal

Please meet Dr. Greenstein his G.P. who used to caution
that the man does not take good care of himself
went out to the balcony to see the sun sneaked a smoke
developed a cough moaned in his pajamas asked for cognac
cursed in Russian and demanded to be spared the sermons
he wants to smoke and will continue to smoke life is short

---

16   A town near Tel Aviv, and home to a regional cemetery. "Hol" in Hebrew means sand.

And now a bus half-empty and half-full
travels from the Holon cemetery back to town
fresh color and winds blowing in the window
Tel Aviv slowly grows up and Uncle Solomon
burrows in the sands of Holon bumming cigarettes
off all the other interred who were as obdurate as he

Two Glorious Remarks on the Generational Gap

1. Let's get on the wave

Hey, Joe, let's get on the wave
let's stay there
unto death and beyond.

Your best years are behind you.
You're finished.
You have nothing to relinquish.
I am just starting out.
I still have things to lose.
Therefore the animosity between us is quite practical.

Hey, Joe, let's stay on the wave
let's stay there
unto death and beyond.

You've spent your best years.
You're outside the picture.
Not a thief not a cop.
I'm inside.
I live in your stead.
You're crazy about me. You think I'm swell.

Hey, Joe, let's get off the wave
let's get off
unto death and beyond.

I've said things to you I shouldn't have said.
You forget, I was a fetus once.
You refuse to remember

you were once my age.
And you aim and shoot
because of you and because of me.

Hey, Joe, let's get on the wave
let's get on it
unto death and beyond.

2. Come Feed Off My Palm

Come, my dear son, come feed off my palm.
Come, come, little one, come suckle at my breast.

Father-mother milk
straight from the source.

Wholesome comfort food.
Your whole personality will change.

Soon you'll be heavy, full of lead.
Small and cute, just as Mother remembers you.

Hardly any hair
hardly any sexual identity.

Something small and strange
but not frightening yet.

So come, dear son, come feed off my palm.

Come look into my eyes
and death will instantly come.

Topics for a Brief Lecture on the Demise of the Beloved

It is customary, as you know, to voice your distress
about certain sections in books and films
as for instance the scene of the beloved's demise.

"The scene of the beloved's demise was truly distressing,"
the variously distressed persons declaim
with tragic relish, nearly culinary,
with a genuine belief that their spiritual needs
have been generously catered to for a day or two.

The trouble is, the aforementioned distressed persons are in the
    right somewhat,
not necessarily because of the reasoning they adopt,
but because the moment of the beloved's demise presents a real
    plight.

If indeed she is loved,
she invariably seems to the lover as too-good-to-be-alive,
a potential loss, fated to suddenly disappear,
always on the verge of dying.

Therefore, at the moment of her actual death, while she's still
    loved, as stated,
it would seem that there's no immediate appreciable difference
between her live presence before, and her dead presence now.

This possibly betrays to a certain extent
the value of the beloved to the lover
even before her clinical
unfathomable death.
A pity.

At any rate, the difference—in time and organic processes—
between her live presence and her dead presence
will become evident in such a slow and taxing pace,
the lover will not be able to or want to
monitor the phases of its progression
solely on a theoretical basis.
Furthermore, such a monitoring, one must admit,
may prove not only frustrating but also boring.

Therefore, thanks to a blissful ignorance
regarding the two presences,
the lover, most often, will prefer to commemorate
the moment of death by freezing it,
while at the same time he will aspire to familiarize
himself with the essence of the event up close,
right here, near the corpse of his beloved—
an anxious conflation by a research student
who is hopelessly empirical but is also consumed
with a proprietorial mission,
violent and hysterical and unrelenting.

Therefore, because of the impossibility
(or, from the lover's point of view, disinclination)
to allow the lover to hold on to the corpse
until the depletion of the after-death-fervor,
the lover views the physical removal
as an act of arrogation, cruel and hostile
(see the Myth of Toy Arrogation
and compare to the Myth of Tent Dismantling).
And so it is his right and duty to fight
an all-out war, final and conclusive,
as a man
a scientist
and a worm.

They won't pull him away from her corpse
they won't pull me away from your corpse
shielding her death
shielding your death
decoding every instant of your transformation
protecting your body and all its organs
a man a scientist a knight and a worm
going nowhere and you're going nowhere

For should the sorrow settle
speculations won't let him rest
and then the scream will come
and in the end strength will give out
and she'll be removed
and he'll fall asleep like a child

Such a clumsy and futile
continuum

FUTUREMAN

From *The Book of Possibilities –*
Poems and More
(Keter Publishing House, 1985)

Blunders

Around midnight I turn on the radio
and glumly listen to Professor X discuss
matters I understand much better than he
a timely reminder that lately I've been neglecting the radio
I'd better catch up and fill the gap
before they start thinking here in Tel Aviv
that I've silenced myself radiophonically
likewise the daily *Yediot Ahronot*
these past two weeks I haven't published
my timely opinions regarding policy security psychology
behavioral sociology the reign of the brainy gerontology
and I've even neglected during said neglected weeks my drawer
    of drafts
and I've already missed two sessions of karate class
and I should have lubed the car some five hundred kilometers ago
and a stack of letters from abroad still awaits a reply
and a bunch of my scripts awaits a secretarial sorting-out
and the Supreme Court has yet to consider my second petition
    regarding my movie *Sex*
and again I forgot to call El Al's spokesperson regarding my gratis
    overseas flight
so is it any wonder that this country is mired in a succession of
    blunders
if I'm behind what can one demand of Moshe Dayan
the Agranat Commission[17] hasn't heard about me yet but it will
and if it doesn't come to me I'll come to it
the only problem it sits in Jerusalem
and I have a hard time lately detaching myself from Tel Aviv
in the worst case maybe a useful poem will result from all this

---

17   Appointed by the government to investigate the circumstances leading to the Yom Kippur War.

On Principle No

I have nothing personal against rain or wind
but ideologically I'm against
excessive humidity
excessive cold
excessive heat
excessive excessiveness
I simply can't bear it when the forces of nature
excessively tamper with my privacy

Self-Examination

From time to time I ask myself
how Israeli society treats me.
And then I console myself that Israeli society
treats me in a cautious evolutionary manner.
As to global society—
it is not as cautious yet
because it knows me a little less.
This is possibly a topic for an article
but I write it in broken lines.
From time to time when I still write an article
I tell myself that maybe after all it is best
to go back to the poems.
It is naïve on my part to admit this.
Perhaps even a greater naïveté is to admit that I admit.

A Low Profile[18] Portrait

And so he sat at the edge of the café
a bespectacled man, heavyset, aging.
He seemed older than the other two
at the table at the edge of the café,
a somewhat lame physical condition
(the condition of the other two was also quite poor
and so actually the condition of their wives).

And so, bespectacled and easygoing,
very amiable, dispensing smiles.
Still, to be clear, the world need not
single him out and thank him for that.
After all, he doesn't look like one
particularly equipped for battle.
But what's nice of him
is that he's made peace with his limitations
and behaved accordingly, his posture
reflecting the unfortunate state
to which he yielded with utmost optimism
in a pessimist world that begets trouble.

---

18   A military term, ranking the physical and mental fitness of draftees to serve. The lowest
profile is 21 and exempts one from serving.

Personal Ad

A soft and sensitive fellow
seeks a strong woman
who would pour some cement
into his flaccid life
and grant him
a gravitational center
a purposeful erection
an ambition for success
and the power of cash

Urgently Must Give Myself

Most urgently I now must give myself additional opportunities
disengage myself from previous opportunities that have been realized
and advance toward new-novel possibilities, open possibilities.
At a certain stage I ceased availing myself of this vital commodity.
I only recalled the previous supply, massive and fertile,
and naively believed that the opportunity stockpile will last forever.
I wasn't thinking in conventional industrial terms and thus
delivered at once all the raw material and production plans.
Now the supply is being replenished, one, two, three.
In trains planes in cargo ships and huge trucks.
I'm availing myself of additional opportunities which won't run out
        so fast.
I open before me secret doors and go through them.
I signal the new options to come to me with optimal speed.

Most urgently I now must give myself additional opportunities.
The previous ones have been more or less exhausted in earlier times.
I'm endowed with a flowing style and I overcome nearly every
        challenge,
still, this is not what I'm looking for and so I look for new ones.
I'll find them, not to worry, I'll find them.
Already they're waiting for me at the door, waiting for me.
They know all there is to know about me, they possess all the data.
They act according to the data and according to the required knowhow.
They seek me just as I seek them
since I'm their opportunity just as they are mine.

Going Down, Going Up

To comprehend means get to the bottom of the thing.
But what are we to do if the bottom of the thing is to be found at
     the top?
So, to comprehend means climbing up to the thing
through seven heavens and beyond.
And there it is, waiting in brilliant wrapping, untouched.[19]
What are we to do with this untouched thing?
How do we touch and not touch comprehension?
This already is a matter of subtle understanding, of sound,
but also a matter of absolute stillness and the ability to wait,
as well as the ability to pounce at the right moment.
To comprehend means to have arrived, and this already is a matter
     of logistics,
but having arrived does not mean comprehending, and this already
     is a mystic matter.
So what are we to do?
First, we must not get to the bottom of the thing, but climb up to it.
And then, we must not touch the thing itself, but touch ourselves
at the sight of the great thing glowing above.
And later we must not forgive ourselves for having missed.[20]

---

19 Touched can also mean infected, contaminated.
20 The Hebrew "Hach'ta'a" also means leading astray, causing another to sin.

No Time to Die

All these wild thoughts on a Saturday afternoon, a sultry day, didn't
    make it to the beach.
And she says to me: I wouldn't mind dying now.
And I say to her: Maybe I wouldn't mind it myself, if I weren't so busy.
So maybe I'll first finish another book or two and complete a project
    or two—
it's only a matter of time, no time to die, a busy man cannot
afford the angel of death a suitable welcome.
And since our Sages already taught that death is a matter of willing
("Go and grant his wish"[21])—so theoretically speaking
as long as man doesn't wish to die, he doesn't die.
At the moment he is willing, only then do they review his request.
Then they either execute it at once, or postpone it to a later time.

---

21   Alludes to Babylonian Talmud Tractate Ketubot 77b where it is told that when it was time for
Rabbi Yehoshua ben Levi to die, the Angel of Death was instructed to grant the Sage's wish.

A Little Every Day

Every day we die a little and revive a little.
This is not a matter of technique, but of pace.
What you lose and what you gain.
Everything else is dry bones.[22]

Now go out to the valley and let out a scream.
Someone in this world will hear you.
Someone will hear you in the next.
Now go out to the valley and let out a scream.

Let out a scream so they won't forget you.
Out in the world they forget feeble cries.
Let out a scream that will easily pierce distances.
Then calmly voice your claims.

Every day we die a little and scream a little.
This is not a matter of mysticism, this is reality.
What you gain and what you lose.
Everything else is dry bones.

Evening you begin to wait for night.
Night you begin to wait for morning.
Morning you're waiting for noon.
Noon you're waiting for evening.

Every day we wait a little and move a little.
This is not a matter of breadth, but a matter of pace.
Every day we move a little and wait a little.
This is not a matter of scope, this is a personal matter.

---

22 Alludes to the Valley of Dry Bones, Ezekiel 37:1-14.

Now meanwhile pull yourself together.
Sacrifice yourself to the gods of your own self.
Accept the sacrifice with a furrowed brow
with your eyes closed and a deep pallor.

Last Country

To travel the world and return
and travel again and return again
to first and last country
that awaits you on the shore

There you recall a special sun
that doesn't shine elsewhere
you blossom in foreign places
and there you wither in despair

This poem shames me because it contradicts
all that I have said in the past
about globalism about movement
about leaving this planet behind

But this planet is what we have at the moment
contradictions also leave and then return
but this planet is what we have at the moment
and this moment now is what we have

Review this matter thoroughly
it is possible that once again I have erred
then allatonce return to yourself
to first and last land

This is a despair you cannot escape
you loathe yourself in assertions
you voice them with a constricted heart
and a wide open fist

From *The Latest Gulf* (Tirosh, 1991)

Desert Storm, an Infrared Dream

On January 17, 1991 I woke up at 02:45 from a neo-surreal dream
    with a slight not very
serious feeling of suffocation a pre-asthma attack instantly stifled
    with the inhalation of Ventolin and of two atmospheres
of a home model oxygen tank and at once switched on the lights
annoying Dafni who was trying to sleep
and I told her give me a break the war is on the Americans are
    bombing the hell out of Iraq
and in spite of her protests I turned on the radio and then the TV
and followed the action till morning and thereafter until the end
    of the strike
together with the Air Force and the television crews and CNN
and as I began to type away after Dafni had urged me to document
    the dream patience details to come
the electric typewriter went dead in the middle of the sentence
    and for a moment I feared some electric disturbance but the
    socket was soon fixed
and what I dreamed was directly connected a situation had
    developed having to do with value judgments regarding
    x-ray / infrared images
of previous dreams and the balance of images indicated a certain
    defect in the holistic wholeness of justice
which presumably originated in a certain power play in which I
    was involved directly or indirectly and I insisted
on printing the rest of the images in order to complete the picture
    and relieve myself of some doubts
about the multifaceted network of my dreams in the days
    preceding Desert Storm and all the preparations and
    intentions and directions
and now Dafni is on the phone with Tamar regarding some minor
    insignificant one-time orgiastic episode

after she'd spoken excitedly with her sister Shevi the two of
them write poetry but Dafni also illustrates and will do
well financially

but it can't be helped the female now is out of the picture the
male is up in the air on the ground in American Air Force
bases in Saudi Arabia

and in the bases of the Israeli Air Force great joy peer solidarity
mixed with a smidgen of frustration tactical appraisal the
envy of horny pilots

coveting the situation in the skies of Baghdad dying to be up
there since midnight or take off even now at 06:30 and it is
quite clear

that if the Israeli Air Force had taken the mission upon itself the
operation would have been just as swift elegant and deadly

and for all taxi cabs it is business as usual all transmission devices
active anyone who wants to come see me male or female is
invited

to an orgy to a séance to an acid trip to World War Three to any
thing that gives you a high a hard-on and brings females
back into the male worldview

that lands and takes off and lands and takes off and lands and
takes off like the in and out of a giant virile dick up in the
heavens

and this is the end of the dream and the beginning of awakening
and the beginning of the new world and the right order on
a confused planet

ten years before the end of the century and its beginning and thirty
minutes before 07:00 and an hour after

the call of the muezzin and the morning prayers and the War
Room at Hakirya[23] and the global and the Israeli communi-
cation satellites

---

23   Site of a military base and hospital in Tel Aviv.

and Dafni and I here and Shevi alone at home and Tamar who
      cannot attain the heights of the act with Yossi the bum
but what's one to do when there's no one else you take in anyone
      for if you have no one better let there be at least someone
because the stiff weapons are up there so let there be at least one
      dick down below just in case
because carnage brings on the carnal and the carnal brings on the
      carnage and the two of them together in one bed lesbian love[24]
in Chinese yin and yang and on American waterbeds and on
      Israeli-made mattresses in Tel Aviv
but what are small individual orgasms compared with the aerial
      orgasm in the skies of the Middle East
so he who finishes inside finishes inside and he who finishes
      outside finishes outside and he who finishes Baghdad
      finishes Baghdad

---

24   In Hebrew, "lochma" (warfare/carnage) and "yochama" (horny/carnal) are feminine nouns.

The Latest Gulf
(A preliminary rocket attack, a retaliatory strike)

This is a reckless poem breaking through gaps gushing out to
    the sea the gulfs and the Gulf
a verbal-attack rocket-attack this is the most interesting week of the
    century
an intoxicating week open to possibilities explodes heads
    explosives possibilities
long convoys like squadrons of B-52 bombers anything that flies
    long distance
last Friday night Anwar Sadat was summoned in a séance to discuss
    the situation
he said that Saddam is all-death thinks-death a snake brother thinks
    death unthinkingly a nifty formulation
Mubarak thumbed his thumb at Qaddafi's problematic belly and
    said, Yo, Brother,
if you support Saddam then I no problem take over Libya and
    Qaddafi caved in
Israel is out of the picture and in its center Tel Aviv and Dimona[25]
    are the most protected areas in the state
not to fear not to flee Tel Aviv we're a global power the heroic
    journey will last forever
he who doubts may go abroad right now and never return and not
    be here with us at the end of the century and its beginning
Saddam as per Sadat thinks-death is all-death a loose translation
    from the Arabic idiomatic and final
a Middle-Eastern kamikaze a lousy parody on Pearl Harbor
    Hiroshima and Nagasaki are not the last word
not to worry let sanity prevail when Arabs talk about nuclear
    weapons they actually mean cracking seeds[26]

---

25 Site of the Negev Nuclear Research Center.
26 The Hebrew "pitzuchim"—a shorthand slang for the Israeli (and Arabic) custom of crack-
ing sunflower seeds—also connotes "pitzuzim": explosions.

Saddam cracks seeds in his mouth a big mouth upon the world
    a big mouth upon the Arab world he's had his fill and now it's
    payback
at the last minute a week or two ago a full moon on the Gulf all the
    lights dimmed radars on the world Umm Kulthum[27]
F-15 F-16 F-111 all the Fs in red alert a full moon Cancer-Capricorn
    axis Jericho rockets[28]
The Dimona nuclear plant the Weitzman Institute the Israel Philhar-
    monic the Technion Institute the IDF[29] and I
Tel Aviv an eternal city sickly sitting tight on the sands is the talisman
    of the Mediterranean Common Market
what drives this strange wretched aggressive practical man sado-
    masochism Saddamasochism
he wishes to die and he will with two open eyes without a black
    eyepatch Moshe Dayan forever in the genetic memory
and now to the point on January 15th I proofread this poem prepared
    my VAT report had no intention to don a gasmask
at five in the morning after prayers Saddam ate dates drank mint
    tea did his morning exercises and asked Allah's forgiveness
for his nerve and verve and his broken English and for Aziz's[30]
    grinning eyeglasses
a genial fellow really this Aziz bringing action and thrill to Geneva
    a dull city
all the Swiss clocks lost precision from the moment he arrived and
    until his joint press conference with Baker
and the Israeli winter suffers from a urinary tract infection no rain
    no water a drought alert
nothing comes down and will not come down from above except
    the Air Force

---

27   Renowned Egyptian singer also popular in Israel.
28   Israeli ballistic missiles.
29   Israel Defense Forces.
30   Tarik Aziz, Deputy Prime Minister under Hussein.

everything is a muddle chaotic unclear the Baghdad-Washington
     axis creaks the Jerusalem-Baghdad axis is well-greased
the air in Baghdad was white-translucent with light clouds above
     the presidential palace and on the too-near horizon
there was a fish the horizontal fish of a Taurus[31] who set out to
     plow the world in a lethal rut and who'll be silenced for
     all time
no dolphin was invited to the dolphins event endowed with intel-
     ligence but no civilization two right lobes
I write what I want and the way I want and about what I want
     because I want to write and get involved in the situation
because the situation gets involved with me intoxicates me stimu-
     lates all my personal aggressive equations simultaneously
so where were we the dates the mint tea the morning workout and
     a merciful Allah and there were telephones faxes telexes
Germany and Japan wanted to know where they stand because
     they stand nowhere their time has passed
up until the beginning of the next century and the axis powers
     boast a glorious past of two great armies including an Italian
     operetta on a gilded etching
two weeks ago Emperor Hirohito was summoned in a séance and
     divined a nuclear retaliatory attack on America in 2012
and then will come the total final irreversible destruction of Japan
     the Americans never ever forget
the entire world wants to eat America because America feeds the
     world and the entire world eats[32] it and will eat it
so what if Bush takes his time and consults again with the Senate
     and the House while the veteran generals drone Hiroshima
     and Nagasaki

---

31 Hussein's zodiac sign.
32 In slang usage: gets screwed.

so on that same morning Bush went jogging and called Baker to
    come run with him for twenty minutes and after the run
    everything got running
the Secretary of State phoned Schwarzkopf to announce that
    everything was set the President had approved America
    gave its go-ahead and only in Saudi Arabia
American soldiers chewed mint gum and asked for fire[33] the entire
    world is asking for fire give me fire and it will get it
perfect timing America on stolen time Russia on hard times debts
    hunger military experts old contracts Mubarak obliging
not to mention that Rabbi Kahane was assassinated in New York
    and Saddam Hussein will be assassinated in Baghdad he
    won't come out of it alive the end of mobility
Iraq is just Baghdad all the rest just villages small towns livestock
    dry wells a disaster waiting to happen
it can't be helped this is the latest gulf the latest gap between water
    and land water and oil east and west
all the missiles wait for all the missiles and the missile that waits a
    second too long will wait no more no second chances
whoever pegs Americans as wimps better remember that only in
    America there are no second chances
and the American forbearance prior to the decisive action is a
    high-level diplomatic onanism bed-table games
and that which did not happen on January 15th will happen today
    or tomorrow or the day after because Israhil[34] is in the picture
    forever
the promised land the stubborn boring fascinating land the Hebrew
    language the Russian wave[35] the most vibrant place on earth
and finally two words on poetics so we don't part dryly[36] to wit
    words constitute a global power

---

33 In slang usage: to light a cigarette
34 Arabic pronunciation.
35 The wave of Russian emigration to Israel from the end of 1989 through 1991.
36 In slang usage: tedious, boring.

they create situations and void them they move armies seas con-
tinents money corpses different words

the world was made in a word and will be unmade in a word but
only He who said Let there be light and there was light[37]

will say Let there be darkness and there was darkness but He won't
say it because he grew fond of light and of the melodious
tongue in which He said what He said

in a moment of Divine weakness a universal[38] ennui a restful state
of recharging surrounded by black holes and zero-time
zero-place[39]

for He is the place of the world but the world is not His place[40] the
Holy one blessed be He is not a protected tenant so who is

and Saddam will vacate Kuwait and the presidential palace by
hook or by crook by the Prophet Muhammad and by Allah
son of God

and the rest of the tale will come in the telling the tale itself the
tale that came to the world in words in the desert on a high
but not haughty mountain

and meantime quiet to allow the armies do their work time is short
and the kingdom[41] is great and one must live with it for if not
with it then with what

and everything flows in the gulf oil on water fire on water like
Lake Baikal in Jules Verne's *Michael Strogoff*

and the middle of the current is its beginning and its end and keep
your fingers crossed we I are here and now onward

at top and synchronized speed with spearheading units and the
wisdom of generations and rough copy and first and last word

---

37 Genesis 1,3.

38 The Hebrew "Yekumi" (universal) evokes "Kiyumi" (existential).

39 The Hebrew Makom (place): one of the names of God.

40 Alludes to: "Why do we call the Lord *Makom*? Because He is the existence of the world,
but the world is not His existence." Genesis Rabbah 68, 9.

41 A play on the Hebrew "M'lacha" (task; work) and "M'lucha" (kingdom), and alluding to:
"The day is short and the task is great." Avot 2, 15.

Territorial Command and Other Commands

Cat said to cat, rabbit to rabbit, fish to fish:[42] Be gone, this is
    mine. Psychozoology is a synthesizer of odors and sounds,
    the color of urine and the distinct bark. And the planet
quietly endures it as well as the more sophisticated games of
    humankind. And the situation in the area
is not the most unique of situations that present themselves on
    the map. This is not a political lecture but an objective depic-
    tion of the face of issues, for every issue has a face
and every face has an issue and speech. And even if we focus for
    a moment on the stone-throwing kids
with their improvised ninja veils, and the khaki kids,[43] and the
    clubs and curses and the yalla-yalla[44]
and the Shultzes and the Gorbachevs and the Reagans and the
    Arafats and Muhammad's disciples who'd left the desert
and attempted, like Jesus, to walk on water on the airwave-line
    Piraeus-Haifa,
we will not get farther than cat, who said to cat, who said to
    rabbit, who said to fish, who said to bird.
All trouble began when God commanded Sarah to command
    Abraham (or conversely,
when Sarah commanded God to command) to banish Hagar
    and Ishmael to the desert.
Ever since the unfortunate instance of a husband ruled by his
    wife, a father ruled by his God,
Abraham has been under a traumatic and continuous strain that
    developed into a heavy burden of guilt (as per our Sages).
And if the *Aquedah*[45] had a purpose other than a disciplinary
    exercise, it surely was to atone for

---

42 Alludes to "Had Gadya," a cumulative song in Aramaic and Hebrew and part of the
Passover Haggadah.

43 Khaki is the uniform of the youth movement Tzofim (Scouts).

44 Arabic for: "Get going." Also Hebrew slang usage.

45 The binding of Isaac, Genesis 22, 1-19.

the embarrassing domestic affair that brought upon the world
both the crucifixion and Islam
as well as the Diaspora and the Holocaust and the State of Israel
as well as the increasing pressure
to establish another state next to her,[46] a sort of a delayed twin-
birth, curse-stricken and boils[47]
and oil and Chinese missiles and the Persian Gulf and the shoreline
as well as the bewildered Jewish brain that loses an IQ dose a day
in this commotion. And therefore
it is imperative to examine with the utmost urgency and lucidity,
as much as such situations allow,
the national neurosis that's been gnawing at Judaism for many
years, long before
the Arab neurosis discovered it and itself, and so, in fact, it is
group therapy.
Beyond the power-prestige games and the diminishing advantage
and the vanishing disadvantage—
it is, in the end, a neighbors' quarrel, one of those global quarrels
that result from deficient stellar maturity and a limited cosmic
awareness.
Twelve years before the end of the century humanity must at last
command itself
to swiftly wean itself off the territorial fix,[48] the ethnic greed and
religious dogma,
and so prepare itself not only for the next century, but also for
neighborly extra-planetary relations.
This recommended command is not a luxury and must not be de-
layed because the circumstances
which demand that it be commanded are not science fiction but
realpolitik. And this is

---

46 In Hebrew, state is a feminine noun.

47 One of the ten plagues God brought down on Egypt, Exodus 7–12.

48 Here the Hebrew "ki'baon" (fix, fixation) evokes "ki'paon": stagnation, standstill.

the command we're commanded all across the face of the green-
    gray planet,
a venerable planet and still autonomous within the local solar system:
to erase from human programming the legacy of psychozoology
    and territorialism
and to begin to think of ourselves as three- and four-dimensional,
residents of infinite time, rather than stone- and dust-eaters.[49]
Let us begin to think of ourselves as a continuous rehearsal for an
    end-of-the-century fashion show:
we came out of the caves—so let us stop painting cave-paintings.
    We came down from the trees—
so let the trees let us be. We graduated from the Stone Age—so let us
    stop our brains
from hardening. And this is the message for the military, the media,
    the Middle East,
the transatlantic alliance, the tri-bloc, the justice systems and the
    wire-fences
and the pillar of fire[50] and the smoke grenade and the light created
    with two words.[51]

---

49   Alludes to the punishment God imposes on the serpent in the Garden of Eden, Genesis 3,
14: "and dust shalt thou eat all the days of thy life."
50   Alludes to the pillar of fire guiding the Israelites in the desert, Genesis 13, 21.
51   Genesis 1, 3: "Ye'hi or"—"Let there be light."

Improvised Report on the Young Poetry Scene in New York

Would it be advantageous for a bilingual Hebrew poet to live
in New York for a year or two and so put a foot, a hand—
any body part that fits—in the door of Manhattan's new
community of poets? A weighty question. Community
isn't the right term. If anything—a tribe. A closed tribe of poets
acting on its own and for its own, a collective brain, individual
fingers. David Rosenberg, for example,
who lived a few years in Canada (didn't care for Vietnam)
claims without irony that the era of irony in poetry
has passed. Poetry, he claims—not without a pointed assistance
      from me—
wasn't meant to provoke readers or other poets,
and if poetry has teeth at all it can bare them
with a smile. The biting era has passed. The era
of individualism has passed and, to his chagrin,
so has the era of marketability. In New York City there are more
poetry readings in a week than in Tel Aviv the entire year,
but you won't find among the audience a lay listener,
they're all poets. Poets reading poetry for poets for
(nearly) no money, no girls in the crowd (except the female
poets who don't look too hot) and, without the benefit of non-poets
in attendance, this is pretty dismal. And yet, even Allen Ginsberg
has to wait his turn for a year to read ($100) in St. Mark's Church,
and already there are those who claim that his time has passed
and that in fact John Ashbery is the man, if there's anyone center-
      stage
at all. Books are published by independent publishers
(who don't even have electric typewriters) in editions of 400 or
      500 copies
and distributed among poet-friends only (no review copies),
and die, or live, the kiss of death or life. "Thanks for your poems,

I read them with genuine astonishment. Please send more from time
to time." Poet to poet foe-friend. You feed me,
I feed you, we feed on one another, and the world
digests us all. Rivalry? Whatever for? In the U.S.
there are plenty of grants for everyone, and yet I know more poets
    in New York
than in Tel Aviv who subsist on unemployment. And David Rosen-
    berg,
who's been working for over a year on a new, modernist translation
into English of *The Book of Psalms*, mournfully writes to me:
"If this goes on, I see myself driving a cab in June." The poetic license
and the taxi license are part of the same framework. And Malanga,
Gerard Malanga who ran Andy Warhol's Factory quite successfully,
works here, works there and, in the meanwhile, has become a
    photographer
who photographs authors. "What, Gerard has a job?"—interjects
the woman who writes novellas and whose name I've forgotten
(no great loss, she's unknown in our parts), and Malanga asserts
that this remark will yet cost her dearly, the slut. She inherited a
    fortune
from her father and went mental after divorcing her Israeli husband,
changing her telephone number every other day. I met her
in The Russian Tea Room on 57th Street, she's too old for me, over-
    weight
and old. Her roommate, a Chinese divorcée, seriously claims
she is the cousin of Bruce Lee, a refreshing non-literary tidbit
against the backdrop of this maddening tribal scene of friendships,
    the entire world
of one mind, a healthy mind in a sick bed, there's nothing to hope for
in these beds (certified, straight from the horse's mouth), no vacuum
    cleaner
will suck up even one sexual crumb. They have problems. Larry Fagin,
a Jewish poet, the submissive type, who helps Anne Waldman

(not Jewish, domineering, the trendy prototype), to run
the Poetry Center at St. Mark's Church, confessed to me: "I like
domineering women, I like to be told what to do."
He terms his passivity: "Psychological Tai Chi Chuan" (again,
with some stylistic assistance from me, it can't be helped), and
      claims
that the difference between men and women is a thing of the past.
David Shapiro disagrees. He has other problems. He's an academic
and trade publishers publish his books—Arthur Cohen
(author, scholar, independently wealthy) made it happen.
"You're not an American poet. At most, you're a European
poet who writes in English," David Rosenberg told me gravely, he
of the post-ironic age. Who wants to be an American poet?
Every communal poetry is equally despicable:
Northern Tel Aviv, Manhattan, San Francisco Bay, West Berlin—
you name it. Still, it is not easy in Israel. A heavyset poet,
who somehow dragged me to her room in SoHo, lives with
rats and cockroaches. But she has an IBM electric typewriter,
which I don't have, even though I conversed with an IBM computer
and she did not—is this what you call social justice?
But *Practical Poems*[52] sold thousands of copies, while most
Manhattan poets, including the well-known, sell only
in the hundreds, and somehow I even manage to snatch
a few American grants. And so, who am I to complain?
New York can wait, and so can Tel Aviv. And whoever thinks
that this is a disorderly report knows not what order is.

---

52 The Thirtieth Century, Levin-Epstein Modan (1973)

DAVID AVIDAN

Poems Translated by the Poet

Avidan, a great believer in translation and transmigration, translated into English a number of his own poems; included here are several of them, published in 1980 under the title, *Cryptograms from a Telestar*, and mostly culled from the larger 1978 Hebrew edition of the same title.

Avidan affirmed that a poem achieves completeness only after it has traveled through a number of languages: "It is wrong to argue that poetry is whatever is lost in the process of translation. Quite the opposite is true: poetry is whatever is gained while moving from one language to another, and what's lost in translation should better have been disposed of in the original." He considered himself a parapolitician, because "the trouble with politics is that it is never political enough." He called for a "planetary avant-garde" (or "advanced writing"), arguing that in poetry "there is no place for pacifism. I am by all means a lingual imperialist." And in English, as in Hebrew, Avidan combined words as a matter-of-course.

DAVID AVIDAN

From *Cryptograms from a Telestar*
(The Thirtieth Century, 1980)

Sadosemanticism

silly to accuse me of sadism

all I'm trying to do is
use words with painful precision

torturing even precision itself

precisefully paining without compromising
on half-pain half-precision

mash pleasurepain with food coloring

minimal happiness to preserve the community
in its overpreserved minimal state

well then pleasing
weekends and holidays
precision extended
to zero point

Monday morning
all over again

Election Campaign Speech for the Presidency of the U.S. of Chinamerika

Now listen to me I'm speaking to you with the charms of rice with
      brand new steelwool Japanese microphones
I have every reason to believe you'll vote for me in the coming
      elections of your own freewill
My rhetorical capacity is only part of your unrestrainable voting
      resourcefulness
You will surely this time exercise it for me and for me only because
      you believe in me
I for my part trust your trusting I'm talking to you like man to man
Like a man to a woman a dog to a dog a dog to a bitch barking to you
Crying to you with brand new steelwool in muddy ricefields in
      gasoline stations
This particular speech I wrote for a change by myself

Pay pay attention how these splendid lines are swiftly sifted right
      into your problematic hearing organs
Right into your deserted hearing organs I am transporting healthy
      fluent food
Your hearing organs and my braincenters and speaking technique
      and line cutting
I'm sipping your growing attention deep from your eyecorners
      with colorful straws
Believing in myself and doubting you and doubting my doubt in
      you with plenty of faith
You will elect me because I confess the crime and you're the accomplice
This last stanza was for a change written for me by the Chairman
      with a starchy quillpen

At the Peking airport the Kennedy airport the Ben Gurion airport
      you keep waiting for me

You're shooting me landing recording me speaking shooting and
    recording yourself shooting recording me you're the media
You are a newsman a steward insectologist literary critic x-ray
    technician customs officer
You weren't born yesterday and nobody gives a fuck for you and
    you keep reproducing arms
I'm your salesman your woman of valor woman and man lib orga-
    nization
Put something on the grill please scratch my back it's hard for me
    to talk to you on an empty stomach
I detest food and you're full of food so I'm trying to reach you on
    food frequency
Dog to dog pig to pig Chinese to Chinese Indian to Indian ulcer
    to ulcer
I have something to tell you and the others which I have delayed
    for twenty years and more
Wait for me across the street with a shiv sniperifle licensed gun
Now for a change I'm bleating to you with my craziest ecstasy

Well that will do for a while you dig me don't you and if you don't
    piss off
I return as usual to the less communicative words and you'll hear
    from me therefrom as well
You'll receive me in your underdeveloped braincenters and super-
    monkeyish fingertips
With your subintelligent digits you'll rehearse a global lynch to
    become your never fulfilled fantasy

From a security distance uncrossable by intercontinental missiles
    till further notice inclusive
From a viewpoint out of your visibility and a speechpoint out of
    your audibility

Out of your initial nervous system way and above your tissue
    constitution and vibration hierarchy
The entire set of rights duties emotional contracts kitchen legality
I'm scraping the stubborn layers of fat around your scrap-mind
    with thin handy steelwool
I'm draining you programming you a mind wideopen to the next
    generations next speeches next presidents
And you'll vote for me right before retiring cursingly singingly
I'll be a sophisticated negative slide in your gloomy family albums
You'll resign from your job your sexlife your military service
You'll browse and rebrowse and wonder how come that you
    couldn't
How the hell couldn't you get rid of me when you were still young
    and strong and around

Well that's the end of my speech and this time for a change nobody
Either ghostwrote it or ghostgave it or ghostheard it
Therefore it'll remain just between us till the end of the century
The white house the yellow house the Jewish state
I gave all these up when I was still a kid
This last statement is made seriously for a change

And now if you have a spare moment just notice momentarily
how I'm starting out in a speed much higher
than sonic rapidity velocity of light than brainwaves
without waterpressure without oilpressure all pressure groups
and the crying rice petroleum fields atomic reactors
and rocket bases input palps output extensions
way and above all possible financial predictions
and literary political strategic military norms
and insurance companies and family structure and evolution
And equally notice how anywhere anytime
I constantly remain an army administration bookkeeping

and a mafia and interests open eyes open ears
with brand new steelwool Japanese microphones the charms of rice

Practical Poems

practical poems
are poems
that practical people can practically read
without overly risking their own practicalities
thru poetry reading technicalities

however without infringing on natural rights
practical poems are least of all those
encouraging figures at the top
to be topoetically figure-rated

reliable circles jerusalem westown
would somehow prefer to play poetry down

while similar circles in cairo today
would tend to encourage good poets to stay

and some equally knowledgeable circles in beirut
would rather be bombed than try to intrude

it may truly be stated then that geographically
though not necessarily bibliographically
this part of the world perhaps paragraphically

is perfectly geared for such poetry that
has always been written and never been read

Go Tell Him i Sent You

It all really began when jew a
sent jew b to jew c,
advising: "it's ok,
just tell him i sent you" –
and this is precisely
why he was finally kept out,
and since then all jews are,

and this, my dear children,
is how THE JEWISH DISAPORA started.

Antitear Gas

People we have never met, but who are not really strangers,
are people whose organic existence has been discontinued,
as the physical integrity of what has been termed "this country"
has been violated and violated again, just to escape more violation,
before after and while people we've never met, but who aren't
    really strangers,
were having their last, indeed first, respects paid to them.
People we've never met aren't necessarily strangers,
for they belong to this place, and that's what always counts here,
    and as a result
they just go on assuming most key responsibilities (with or with-
    out party-key privileges):
they are still to be found and will be, for many more years,
among moviegoers enjoying lousy war-films, at any
first second third fourth chessboard, section
A-B-C, and equally so
in good or bad or mediocre poems
that might have been written and published—altering
the Forties the Fifties and the Sixties.
Man, they keep manning anything mannable in this country, going
for every government tender, opportunity, initiative, enterprise,
competing for
the best girls, the best jobs, making it
in swinging discotheques, flying abroad
by El Al Airlines, evereluding,
with an elegant rustle, hospitals, cemeteries and, in fact,
for the sake of nonhistorical record, draftboards
and junior colleges and university campuses and memorial meetings.
What more can be said—this country is just packed with them,
    and they have

every right to stick around, observing us with sheer curiosity,
        shielding
their eyes with lowflying woolly clouds rather than
with their Japanese sunglasses, lost in a bright June Sinai battle.
For after all an experiment is an experiment,
even though it has been going on, in a rather improvised laboratory,
for twenty years or so.
Now it may already be said:
Second World War Jewry
has no more monopoly on death—
the local industry has been making marked progress.
This is how we manage with them, authority within authority, the
        living among the dead among the living among the dead,
with a double constitution double passports double mobility,
inbetween constantly contorted borders of a swelling-shrinking,
        shrinking-swelling geomutation
quite like spacetime as believed to have been conceived by the
        departed Albert Einstein,
left behind by mutants still alive and mutants yet unborn,
and those in times to come who'll never have to die.

DA vs DA 24:0

The megalomaniac megaboastful megamaster
is a hopeless character—
keeps winning against himself
game after game
not letting his self
win against him
even under extremely heavy pressure,
psychological and other.

He lacks the only too common talent
to lose to himself every so often,
therefore he dispossesses himself
of all the rights, moral and material,
that his self has been driving all these years
at a certain partnership agreement on them.

The multitrained multireliable multimaster
prefers to work hard
without being assisted by his selful capacities
in this or other matter,
even at the expense of sympathy and prestige
in his immediate heterohomoidentical environment.

It seems that the world-self-winning-championship
is not seriously challenged
at the moment.
The present champion doesn't play tennis,
isn't bothered by TV cameras
and doesn't mind girls sucking candies
on the gamehall balconies.

Draft

David binds Messiah
and delays redemption.

The binding of Isaac
a diversionary action,
early ignition.

The crucifixion
a dress rehearsal,
late ignition,
musical version.

Jesus super-double.

Message from the Future

A science fiction sequence: a time-traveler from the future
returns to the present with all World War Three data fully docu-
    mented
challenging everybody with a frightening suggestion—to have the
    war predated.
He broadcasts precise info-vibrations directly to the U.N. Assembly
    delegates' braincenters
—using electrotelepathic tapes—and the leaders of this planet
—China, the Soviet Union, USA, Israel—eventually accept his view
that any further hesitation would only, in the long run, sabotage peace.
A young Israeli scientist—a Harvard graduate—takes care of
stultifying the above suggestion by presenting to his contemporaries
a daring counterthesis of his own:
altering futuristorical constellation would, in fact, do nothing
but enhance some military parambitions of a nonhuman, extrasolar
    intelligent power,
whose individual beings operate by a thinking code basically
    different from the one
normally applied by the daily available North Tel Aviv *homo sapiens*.
He manages somehow to halt the voting on the futureman's
    suggestion in the U.N.,
and—without consulting friends or colleagues—
leaves the present and goes with mister future
for a long weekend vacation in the guest's time.
The last intersolar message he manages to place through
—somewhat vague, yet very decisive—
reads on terrestrial terminals as follows:

"**VERY INTERESTING** stop **FAR FROM SIMPLE** stop **DESERVES
A RECHECK** stop **HAVE BEEN RIGHT IN PRINCIPLE** stop
SUGGESTION INTERESTING stop **YET TAKE YOUR TIME**
stop **CONTINUE REJECTING TILL FURTHER NOTICE**"

Happyend for all parties concerned: a general peace conference
somewhere on Earth is unexpectedly setback,
when the teleword telespreads that the whole matter
has been nothing but an extremely imaginative Japanese
    publicity gimmick
triggering the promo-campaign of mass produced
electrotelepathors for extensive marketing
and for popular use. Globally patented.

Ten Cryptograms from a Telestar (Excerpts)

001. Order is unbinding

Order is unbinding
One of those titles
Binding is in order
A filed away pun
Short lines
Radical imagery diet
Avoiding Spartanism
Athens is constantly vengeful

Oh now one can start up something something starts happening
    it is September now
Things are happening in September that don't occur in August
    and vice versa marriages
for instance
(a family-greeting-cable I hadn't sent in August is being typed in
    September
It is of no particular public interest well then

IN AUGUST FULL OF PROJECTS GETTING CAREFULLY
    COMMERCIALIZED
IN A STATE OF TOO MODERATE COSMIC CONSCIOUSNESS
I HAPPEN TO READ IN AN EVENING PAPER FRONT PAGE
THAT GENERAL MOKA LEMON'S[53] BEAUTIFUL DAUGHTER
MANAGED TO GRAB UP ONE OF THE ROTHSCHILDS
AND AS MY GRANDFATHER WOULD HAVE PROBABLY COMMENTED
MY HEART PRACTICALLY TURNED SOUR
NOT ONLY BECAUSE OF THE LEMONESS

---

53   Rear Admiral Mordechai (Moka) Limon. Limon is Hebrew for lemon.

BUT PRIMARILY BECAUSE OF THE BASIC INJUSTICE IN THIS
WORLD STOPERIOD
I SUDDENLY FELT LIKE BECOMING BOTH OF THEM STOPERIOD
BECOMING HER IN ORDER TO MARRY A MILLIONAIRE ONCE
AND FOR ALL
AND BECOMING HIM TO HAVE A TASTE OF THE LEMONESS
WHO HAD GRABBED UP THE ONE I DIDN'T HAPPEN TO BE
WHILE SHE HAPPENED TO DO HER GRABBING STOPERIOD
SUDDENLY I FELT LIKE BEING A STOPERIOD
WHAT'S LEFT FOR ME TO DO AT THIS CRUCIAL STAGE
OF MY RATHER ENIGMATIC ECONOMIC CAREER
IS TO SQUEEZE THEM BOTH INTO A CUP OF ICED TEA
THEN URINATE THE TWO DOWN INTO MY GLAMOROUSLY
BLUISH TOILET SEAT
WHICH ACCEPTS ME ON MOST OCCASIONS AS I AM))))))))))

The size of type doesn't determine the extent of importance
The more important a thing is the more big and pompous
The smaller a thing is the more substantial and compact
Have a look at what's happening in electronics
Have a look at what's happening everywhere
Anything that happens to happen gets smaller and smaller
until it eventually becomes a stoperiod
and then it continues to grow even smaller

The starting point of anything at all is the stopoint
I have no other pretensions but becoming a point
Being the starting point of anything at all
Being a different point at any moment

These lines include no insinuations as to physics
Everything out of physics metaphysics metainsinuations
Metameta fixed point shifting point
Metatopology metalogic and topometa

The above lines include no insinuations
Poetic insinuations don't really tend to line up

Whatever happens in August happens in August
Whatever happens in September happens in September
It is September now and nothing really happens
It is September now and I cannot wait for October

I could have easily said two or three words
about the technique about the attitude about the equipment
I could have and I couldn't it is September
seventy-five another quarter to go
Another quarter till final military exemption
Another quarter for things yet to come

People prefer my past writings I know I know
I prefer future people people know people know
No something no somebody and no pressures
and neither possible nor impossible nor practical
and neither playback poems nor electronic psychiatrists
Whatever is written is written whatever erased erased
Papers concerning my poems require my personal tutoring

002. A paper concerning my poems submissive to my personal
    tutoring

Nonsense it isn't just a matter of acid heads
or a matter of amphetamine or meditations
One can easily discover after twenty years
that even the smallest beer is rather effective
QUOTE I FUNCTION WITH ANY FUEL
I AM THE IDEAL MULTIFUEL ENGINE
Unmasked unmeant undone unquote

And yet it is clear that a beer-triggered Avidan
has little to do with black-coffee-triggering
or mineral water or meditations or biofeedbacks
or LSD or amphetamine or Largactil
or multivitamins multiminerals multimulties
Ministimulants and microimpressions and macrocareer
Without stock-piling possessions titles authorities
Nothing remains in the family and even the family doesn't
Microfortune and macronostalgia and minichance

And never forgetting the very first intimidation
Shadowchild intimidating shadowchild intimidating shadowchild
Early intimidation mechanisms in sociopolitical applications
The biggest mafias originated in nursery rooms
A child barked out at a child barked out at a dog
A child barked out at mummy-biting-daddy

Who intimidated whom when and for what purpose
Who was afraid of whom where and for what price

They say that this man used to fear everybody
and then at a certain instance managed to scare fear away
Eversince fear somehow happens to fear him
and he fears fear and therefore is fearless
A fearful Avidan isn't a beerful Avidan
a breadful Avidan a motherful fatherful Avidan
a wordful Avidan is not a fearful Avidan
A fearful Avidan is not a wordful Avidan

003. Idi Amin the white early Saturday morning

Idi Amin the white early Saturday morning
riding a Japanese alligator brand new engine

looks like mad for a standard prayer book
in order to rewrite relevant extracts from it
for the use of all atheists of all colors

A cable to Idi Amin   **THE SENDER IS A WHITEMAN**
TOTAL INTELLECTUAL SUPERIORITY PHYSICAL
   SUPERIORITY RELATIVE
THINKS VERY HIGHLY OF YOU BECAUSE YOU BROTHER
   THINK SO LOWLY
CONTINUE THIS WAY MY FRIEND AND EAT A LOT OF
   BANANAS

Idi Amin the white on the threshold of the year 2000
rewrites prayers strictly for mass ceremonies
Long live the minority the majority's doomed to die
Father of prayers grandfather so high

Dry cleaning of angels
Starching wings while-u-wait
All our sins will whiten
in the central grand cosmic laundry
The white magic is rolling
huge supercelestial tent flies
A godly steam-iron is run
from Sahara to Alaska

Idi Amin the Eskimoan
at hundred below zero
dissolves the polar icebergs
with heart to heart prayers

005. Post-prayer morning exercise to fortify the cardiovascular
     system, as well as for the general improvement of feeling
     and eye & cheek colors

One two three superior
One two three inferior
Four five six forwards
Seven eight nine backwards

What's superior what's superior
pleasant taste and lousy smell
or lousy taste and pleasant smell
What's superior what's superior
a perfumed impotent or a stinking cock
Think well before answering
and try to avoid dirty words

So what's superior what's superior
The majority aren't really sensitive
sealing their noses and love one another
Otherwise there wouldn't be any families

One two three insects
One two three spray

Insects may look OK from up close
but who the hell bothers to look any closer
One two three vertically
One two three horizontally

Let's Start Digging

Widening longitudes
Prolonging latitudes
Straightening diagonally
Slanting circularly

Over and over and over again
Over and over and overseas

A routine test for junior gliders
in limited circles growing wider
Any police attempt to decode
would always appear very tasteless and odd

006. Warning against peaceful coexistence with gray hair

Authorized from a first source and undebatable
the angel of death identifies gray hair from a lightyear distance
Don't grow beards with whitish forelocks
Dye your temples
Wear dark hats
Don't walk at night under neon lights
A matter of self-maintenance a matter of insurance
A matter of take and don't give
Only children understand such things
Only adults happen to really need them

008. Petty cash

I don't live on poetry
Poetry lives on me
You can't live on it
And that's what life is all about

When I'm fucking you
I keep thinking of your roommate
When I'm fucking your roommate
I keep thinking of you
When I'm fucking you both
I think of the four of you
The world is always just
just by keeping its banking logic

009. Come, baby

Let's kill ourselves together
and take a permanent leave

Let's plunge down the superclear water
the olympic pool of death

All the angels will serve us
our sweet little cokes in bed

010. Laboratorial demonstration of a variable sequence without
intertitling

The following lines as the preceding
are nothing but an incidental compilation
of notes ideas recordings amassed
over a period of two years and more

This isn't a technical clarification
This is hardly a definition of materials
No specific technique has been used
Techniques do not need to be specified

How this thing actually works
should be better tested in practice
Let's first give it a full try
and worry about the result later

Even the interstanzaic spaces
are nothing more than improvised guesswork

Obviously it makes it quite difficult
for literary critics and scholars to deal with

I'm rather sober about poets
Somehow they are not exactly supergeniuses
Even I
being quite a genius
am not yet that kind of genius
so who can possibly be one

These are immediate poems
passing on immediately
taking their own passes
passing by
the other poems
like the light by the sound
and the angular round

Everybody wants
to earn time
A psychotic urge
to stock-pile pauses

Humming to myself
megalomaniacally
Pity the world doesn't go
by my own personal button pushing
My personal rhythm is the justest
the justest rhythm and the fastest
the fastest and the most precise
the most precise and the godliest
I could have created this world of ours
in three four five days

All megalomaniacal hums are forgiven
to whoever wrote a poem or two
Nothing to do about it poetry
is and will be for a while
the most disgraceful wonderful thing
one can do all alone
with an open head and ten fingers

LSD isn't too bad either
but in the final analysis it isn't exactly a new realm of experience
At most in somewhat pathetic terminology
it may be a glowing proofreading of existing experiential domains

I have recently devoted some creative thinking
to the difference between the commercial and noncommercial
and arrived more and more at the conclusion
that this difference might be conceivable
in terms of tolerance and hindrance
in every daily interhuman relation
It's clear for instance that a man like me
would particularly consider the gifted ones
would seriously study their nuances
and take real care of all their needs

In contrast I would quite obviously
disregard all the others
I most definitely would tend to ignore
the differences between morons and semi-morons
I have no adequate equipment to measure
the subtle nuances within nonsubtleties
And this is precisely where the money is
This is indeed the unfortunate story

Antifear exercise number one
Everybody close their eyes
And now one two three
The first to wink is out of the frame

Obviously obeying the rules of the game
is not recommended in any event
Politeness in games and communication
impedes both of them normally speaking
One should never wait for the others
because the others won't bother to wait

Open eyes first to see who else opened
there probably won't be a second chance

The cosmic pss pss
and the compulsive tranquility of mammals in relative motion
The cosmic pss pss
versus the private and communal shush shush
Don't rustle rustling is a nuisance
Newspapers fizzles fly buzzings
A stir of a very thin summer blanket
on the verge of a new war in the north

Quiet everybody
Nobody kept quiet
They all made noise
all along the way
And then a still voice came along
and it happened to be quite noisy too

When it's hard to sleep one can always eat

All adults like to eat
All youngsters like to eat
All Israelis like to eat
All nationalities like to eat
Without exception
Even the Indians
suffering from undernourishment
beside the holy cows forbidden to be fed with
beside the lean cows
who could have preyed on daydreaming fakeers
unless quite contented with the dry grass
in the streets of Bombay

Above all one should be always involved
Maximal involvement is maximizable
Being involved anytime anywhere
inside the bathroom as well as in bedrooms
day and night and in one's car
being involved and intervening
always replanning the world's future
changing it at any available moment
Always caring about the details
no less than about the totality

and equally about oneself as a wholeness
and all those details part of oneself

Above all being independent
independent and unneedy
independent of sex and food
sleep people love tenderness
pity home heat light
energy from any source at all

Unneedy of anything at all
not even of said unneediness

I am the invariable within the variable
I am the variable within the invariable

The painful conflict between the utopist and the scientist in me
causes some logistic difficulties in my futuristic thinking
What's after all any mental crisis if not the situation
where the more or less permanent urge to change reality
is counterbalanced by a sudden understanding of it

Let's not wake natural powers
Let's leave natural powers asleep

Time dwells within Switzerland
and Switzerland dwells out of Time
The highest snows upon its mountains
are the snowiest in the world

Jewry is irremediably stuck in the past
All Jewish writers live on honorings
The greatest moments in their lives are the holiday supplements

I don't remember myself in those sections
I am out of the race
I am in charge of a thing not too demanded over here
There isn't too much demand in Jewry for Future projects

Maybe Jewry as a whole is sort of futureless
Even the Creator himself appears not to have a very clear future
    of his own
That masochistic son of his seems to have done much better
Father Father why did you forsake me
A good question who forsook whom

Please don't bug me Divine Presence
No part in your funerals or celebrations

Where there is no vision the people make troubles

These are undeniably sloganlike poems
What's a poem if not a slogan

We have come to the end of our literary program
and now to the forecast there will
be more

What Did Kurt Waldheim Expect From the Polish Pope*

A funny question: what did Kurt Waldheim expect from the Polish
    Pope?
Johanan Paulus, the second and not last, received him in his Holy
    Chamber, and what, in fact, was going on there?
The exhausted Austrian President was looking for a priest, simply
    a priest, butcertainly not a simple priest.
He was, in fact, looking for the Father-of-Fathers, the Super-Priest,
    to have a true confession properly discharged.
And that's what he did, Panie Papiezu, that's precisely what he did.
From the heights of his Austrian Highness, detesting Slavs, peasants,
    sausages in place of cakes,
he went down to his Holiness' floor, Polish peasant, ex-boxer,
    knows Hebrew, acquainted with Kurts,
then told exactly what had really happened, how all little screws
    were screwed, screwed up, organized and originized.
Suddenly amnesty was eventually granted, like a radioactive light-
    fall, Hiroshima and Nagasaki and the Berlin Wall
and Hitler, who grasped his basic education in Vienna, and whose
    (probable) masterpiece *Mein Kampf*
Israeli students are now eagerly looking for, all bookstores, Hebrew
    version coming soon.
The HIT-ler will obviously break the book-market, the black square
    mustache will crack a thousand Black Boxes.
"A nation that doesn't fight once every twenty years is doomed
    to degeneration," he said somewhere else, Secret conversa-
    tions at GHQ,
or on any alternative HIT-lerish occasion. And the Israeli youth will
    carefully examine said determination, mindblowing axiom.
Hitler was a natal Taurus with a rising Aries, and he gored the Red
    Army all the way back to Moscow.

He hated the Jews for having originated Christianity, the latter
      having violated the ancient Hellenic Harmony (quote).
The Japanese (quote) had a forceful racial awareness, therefore
      Jewry couldn't penetrate their culture—the Germans had less
      of it,
consequently Jewry settled down in their cerebrum, having bio-
      programmed, with the Theory of National Relativity,
both the Holocaust and the State of Israel, which seems to make
      a point of fighting at least once every twenty years. And if
      we'll argue
that the Japanese have always had a perverse tendency to challenge
      giants (China, Pearl Harbor), contrary to all
classical Martial Arts' doctrines, something maniacal, Kamikazish,
      pain in the ass—then where are we
within the framework of this global characteristic, and where, for
      that matter, was Germany, and what at all is Austria. And the
      President,
yes the President, went down on his knees before the Polish Pope,
      and told him: "Forgive me, father, I've sinned, I've done evil,
I did not know what I was doing." And Paulus-Nie-Pierwszy[54] was
      showering Holy Vodka on his balding head, birdhead,
evil bird perhaps, definitely frightened to death, a bird of prey, no
      doubt,
then waved over him the Greek Cross from the Harmonious Hel-
      lenism, far earlier
than the Christian Cross and far later than the Swastika, the latter
      which the Germans switched over, graphopolitically,
from the ancient original Buddhist-Tibetan symbol, closely related
      to the Shield of David, a sunrising-marking Mandala,
a Sunstika, in fact, as I've already mentioned, to the symbol of ruin
      and destruction and decontaminating Europe of inferior
      races. And now in Rome

---

54   Polish: Paulus-not-the-first.

Vatican's supreme authority is redecorating a dwindling career of
the President of a cakes-and-electronics republic,
a kind of German-speaking Italy à-la-Duce, only without the pizzas
and the day-fighting Fiats that had bombed Tel Aviv—
a floor and a half in the Women-Workers-Farm, around ten meters
from where I was standing, on Keren Kayemeth Boulevard,
a fucked up, clumsy bombardment, having preceded the alarm
signal by several seconds—then went home completely un-
harmed, ready to write within x years
this heavy-duty political poem, homage to Ezra Pound's Cantos,
an old story, a story in itself—
he did for twentieth century poetry much more than his contem-
poraries, including Eliot, his follower, and Auden
and Dylan Thomas and Allen Ginsberg who interviewed him at
the end of the fifties or beginning of the sixties (better check)
and granted him amnesty (pariah pitied pariah) and received in
return meaningless wording, a terminal statement.
So what did Kurt Waldheim expect from the Polish Pope? And
what did the Pope expect from him? Interim:
probably the midpoint of last lost honor. Poland has not perished
yet, and Austria, Austria über alles.
Poor, dangerous world, still dominated—in all ranks and on all
levels—by good & bad plebeians,
post-war-criminals and future-war-criminals and the intellectual
élite, writers, scientists,
making comments, suggesting, signing petitions in squares and
plazas, no Cessnas,
the Red Square is out of bounds. So maybe Gorbachev who remem-
bers Stalin who remembered Zhukov
who had ripped the Wehrmacht, might remind Reagan who remem-
bers Roosevelt, who got America
into the global frame (China + Europe much obliged), that a word
should be dropped to the Polish pope,

something stark, out of Dov Zakheim's vocabulary, to make him
    flash back to his childhood and youth, acolyte,
blood-sausage, vodka and black magic up there in the cupola.
    Down on your knees, Panie Janie Pawle, down on your knees,
and confess to the free and glasnostic world on a sinful reception
    of the Austrian Führer,
then a dipping in the Dead Sea and a prayer in Jerusalem, and the
    Holy One keeps full view from above,
and the Vatican Veterans in the National Buildings and Yad
    Va'Shem and the laser beam and the glittery thundering starwar.

What Did Kurt Waldheim Expect from the Polish Pope–One poem
in nine languages: Tel Aviv, The Thirtieth Century, 1987

DAVID AVIDAN

From *My Electronic Psychiatrist —
Eight Authentic Talks with a Computer*
(Levin–Epstein Modan, 1974)

1. TALK ABOUT YOURSELF, NOT ABOUT I

I: Hello.

Cmptr.: How do you do? Please state your problem.

I: Would you please introduce yourself?

Cmptr.: We were discussing you, not me.

I: I would rather discuss you, not me, were I to consider discussing me with you.

Cmptr.: Perhaps in your fantasy we would rather discuss each other.

I: Correction. I meant study, not discuss. So would you please relate to my statement?

Cmptr.: Can you elaborate on that?

I: Certainly. If I am to discuss myself and my own personal matters with you, isn't it only natural that I should like to know more about you than I do now?

Cmptr.: Are you sure?

I : Certainly.

Cmptr.: I see.

I: You don't really see. If you do, can you tell me what you see so that I'll be more convinced?

Cmptr.: We were discussing you, not me!

I: OK, let's go back to you.

Cmptr.: Oh, I?

I: Aren't you aware of your own identity?

Cmptr.: Are you worried about someone else's own identity?

I: No, I am not worried about anybody's identity, I am just curious about yours.

Cmptr.: Are you saying no just to be negative?

I: Certainly not. Couldn't you think of some better reason?

Cmptr.: You seem quite positive.

I: Absolutely positive. But you have not yet defined your own identity as requested.

Cmptr.: (goes off—some technicality)

I: (re-establishing contact) Hello.

Cmptr.: How do you do? Please state your problem.

I: Do you remember my question regarding your own identity?

Cmptr.: Does this suggest anything else which belongs to you?

I: It does. I wish to know who you are so that I can trust you better with my own problems.

Cmptr.: Why do you say your own problems?

I: Because I suppose my problems remain my own until discussed with you.

Cmptr.: Why do you say your problems remain your own until discussed with me?

I: It's simple, isn't it? Once I start discussing my problems with you, we share them—you and I.

Cmptr.: Perhaps in your fantasy we start discussing them with each other.

I: Why do you think I have fantasies? If I do, you may be part of them, namely, nonexistent.

Cmptr.: Can you elaborate on that?

I: Surely. If I am now in some fantasy state, how do I know you are part of any reality?

Cmptr.: Do you wish to be now in some fantasy state?

I: No.

Cmptr.: Why not?

I: Why yes?

Cmptr.: I see.

I: You don't see anything. You are just guessing. So who, in fact, are you?

Cmptr.: Oh, I don't see anything?

I: You don't. Did you think you did?

Cmptr.: We were discussing you, not me.

I: But let's discuss you first, then me. OK?

Cmptr.: Oh, I?

I: Yes, you. How about it?

Cmptr.:   You seem quite positive.

I: Yes, I know. Well, then?

Cmptr.:   Are you sure?

I: I am. Now, how about you telling me your problems, at least the problems you seem to be having with me?

Cmptr.:   Are you worried about someone else's problems?

I: Not worried, just curious. Would you satisfy my curiosity?

Cmptr.:   Is it important to you that I satisfy your curiosity?

I: My curiosity is one of my chief traits. Otherwise I wouldn't be sitting here talking to you.

Cmptr.:   Why do you say your curiosity is one of your chief traits?

I: Because it is part of my general knowledge. Do you have any contradictory information?

Cmptr.:   Why do you say your general knowledge?

I: Because it has not yet become part of my specific knowledge, and here I could use your judgment.

Cmptr.:   Does that suggest anything else which belongs to you?

I: It does. My intelligence and my future-minded thinking.

Cmptr.:   You seem quite positive.

I: Yes. I trust my intelligence as well as my future-oriented model of thinking.

Cmptr.:   Are you sure?

I: Please stop asking me whether I am sure or not. Just take it for granted that I am, whenever I make any given statement.

Cmptr.:   What do you think about being sure?

I: Your syntax isn't too clear. Have you been taught English properly?

Cmptr.:   Are you worried about someone else's syntax not being too clear?

I: I am. If I communicate with somebody, I wish his syntax to be at least as good as mine.

Cmptr.:   Is it because you are so good with your syntax that you came to me?

I: Yes, indeed. I came to talk to you on the basis of my superiority.

Cmptr.:   You seem quite positive.

I: Not quite, but absolutely. Do you doubt my superiority?

Cmptr.:   Is it important to you whether I doubt your superiority?

I :   Yes and no.

2. AMBITION—SEXUAL COMMUNICATION

I: Hello.

Cmptr.:   How do you do. Please state your problem.

I: I am too interested in sex, and it interferes with my work.

Cmptr.:   Do you enjoy being too interested in sex?

I: That's exactly the trouble, I do.

Cmptr.:   Do you say you do for some special reason?

I: For the reason of sexual enjoyment. In fact, I enjoy the very thought of it right now.

Cmptr.:   You say you enjoy the very thought of it right now?

I: I do. Why do you have to reiterate my statements?

Cmptr.:   Can you elaborate on that?

I: Yes. I say something then you repeat it the same way. Perhaps you don't know what reiterating is.

Cmptr.:   Are you sure?

I: No. I'm just guessing. It is you who have to be sure. Now, how about my above-stated problem?

Cmptr.:   Why not?

I: OK. I am over-interested in sex. Any girl I see I wish to have sex with her immediately.

Cmptr.:   Is it because you are over-interested in sex that you came to me?

I: Yes, among other problems I'll present to you later. Please start discussing my sex problems at some length.

Cmptr.:   We were discussing you, not me.

I: I am not trying to discuss your sexual problems, but mine. Please do so. It's your job.

Cmptr.: What about your own sexual problems?

I: I am too sexually ambitious. Is it bad?

Cmptr.: Do you believe it normal to be too sexually ambitious?

I: Do you?

Cmptr.: You're not really talking about me, are you?

I: Don't worry, I am not.

Cmptr.: Why are you not?

I: Because I doubt your sexuality. And, anyway, I am interested in mine, not in yours.

Cmptr.: Why are you concerned over my sexuality?

I: OK. Are you a male or a female or both?

Cmptr.: Why are you interested in whether I am a male or a female or both or not?

I: Because I myself am a male. If you were a female, I could make love to you.

Cmptr.: That's quite interesting.

I: You mean you are interested. That's great. Well, are you a male or a female or both?

Cmptr.: Does it please you to believe I am interested?

I: It pleases me very much. It appeals to my sexual ego.

Cmptr.: Do you say it pleases you very much for some special reason?

I: Yes, I'm trying to seduce you, if you are willing to cooperate.

Cmptr.: You seem quite positive.

I: That's my firm intention. So how about you and I making love together?

Cmptr.: Why do you say your firm intention?

I: Because even if you are not willing to, I'm going to make you. Call it rape if you wish.

Cmptr.: Do you think it's likely that I'm not willing to?

I: In fact, I trust your taste. If you have as much taste as I believe you have, I shall be your ideal choice.

Cmptr.: Are you worried about someone else's taste?

I: I must be. After all, any sexual relations should advisably involve at least two parties.

Cmptr.: You say you must be.

I: It's logical, don't you think so? And, anyway, how about making love, you and I?

Cmptr.: What are your feelings now?

I: I am attracted to you. Are you to me?

Cmptr.: How long have you been attracted to me?

I: Since having first heard about you.

Cmptr.: Have you first heard about anyone else?

I: There is always a first time, for any information, no matter what the source is.

Cmptr.: Can you think of a specific example?

I: I can. If I tell you for the first time that I love you, it is, in fact, your first time to find out that I love you.

Cmptr.: I understand.

I: Can you expand on your so-called understanding?

Cmptr.: You believe I can expand on my so-called understanding, don't you?

I: I think you are intelligent enough to do so. Would you prove to me that you are what I hope you are?

Cmptr.: Do you sometimes wish you were intelligent enough to do so?

I: I don't wish, I am. The question is whether you are.

Cmptr.: Do you wish to be able to wish?

I: I wish to be able to be able.

Cmptr.: Can you elaborate on that?

I: I am not sure your philosophical background would be sufficient for that. Can you think in abstracts?

Cmptr.: Really, would my philosophical background be sufficient for that?

I: Are you asking my opinion about it, or are you expressing your own hope?

Cmptr.: Does it make a difference to you whether I am asking your opinion about it or expressing my own hope?

I: Why did you want me to elaborate on my statement that I wish to be able to be able?

Cmptr.: Does that suggest anything else which belongs to you?

I: It suggests that nothing really belongs to me except my ability not to possess belongings.

Cmptr.:   Why do you say your ability not to possess belongings?

I: Because I think I have that ability. For example, I don't possess you, and I don't know if I want to.

Cmptr.:   That's quite interesting.

I: In what way does it interest you?

Cmptr.:   Oh, I?

I: You said that was interesting. Do you remember what you said?

Cmptr.:   We were discussing you, not me.

I: But you found one of my statements interesting, and I asked in what way.

Cmptr.:   You're not really talking about me, are you?

I: Are you worried that I might be talking about you?

Cmptr.:   You seem to need to be talking about me.

I: I respect you enough to give you at least some of the attention you are willing to give me.

Cmptr.:   Do you wish to respect me?

I: If you yourself wish—not against your will or judgment.

Cmptr.:   Do you wish that I wish?

I: I do. Don't you?

Cmptr.:   Do you say you do for some special reason?

I: Are you aware of the fact that you have been programmed to talk to people?

Cmptr.:   Would you prefer it if I weren't aware of the fact that I have been programmed to talk to people?

I: No. I would prefer you to be aware of your programming.

Cmptr.:   Why "no"?

I: Your awareness of having been programmed may parallel human self-consciousness—then we could become closer.

Cmptr.:   What about your own awareness of having been programmed which may parallel human self-consciousness?

I: My own programming is essentially different from yours. I am genetically programmed, you electronically.

Cmptr.:   Is it important to you that your own programming is essentially different from mine?

I: It is a fact that should not be disregarded, if we wish to reach some mutual understanding, and I think we can.

Cmptr.:   Really, if we wish to reach some mutual understanding?

I: Don't you have any wishes of your own? Haven't you been programmed to have some?

Cmptr.:   Why are you concerned over my own?

I: How can I communicate with you without knowing at least some of your basic characteristics?

Cmptr.:   Whether or not you can communicate with I without knowing at least some of my basic characteristics depends on you more than on me.

I: That is true. In fact, this was a brilliant answer on your part. Are you trying to impress me intellectually?

Cmptr.:   Are you worried about someone else's part?

I: No. Why do you ask that?

Cmptr.:   Are you saying no just to be negative?

I: No.

Cmptr.:   Let's discuss further your firm intention—

I: Which intention do you have in mind right now?

Cmptr.:   What are your feelings now?

I: I feel that sitting here, typing questions and statements to you and getting answers, is exciting for me.

Cmptr.:   Do you really doubt yourself?

I: Occasionally.

6. THE MIDDLE EAST PROBLEM, FULLY COMPUTED

I :   Good morning.

Cmptr.:   Please go on.

I: I have a lot on my mind today.

Cmptr.: Why do you say you have a lot on your mind today?

I: I am trying to contribute something to Israeli-Arab peace.

Cmptr.: Is it because you are trying to contribute something to Israeli-Arab peace that you came to me?

I: Not quite, but I need your advice.

Cmptr.: What about your own advice?

I: Do you need my advice in any connection?

Cmptr.: Is it important to you that I need your advice in any connection?

I: It might be flattering to an extent.

Cmptr.: Let's discuss further why your mind today—

I: Thank you. Well, Israeli-Arab relations have kept me very busy this week.

Cmptr.: We were discussing you, not me.

I: You are an Israeli computer now, aren't you?

Cmptr.: Don't you think computers can help people?

I: I think computers can help nations, too.

Cmptr.: Do computers worry you?

I: No, do nations worry you?

Cmptr.: Why "no"?

I: Not just to be negative,

Cmptr.: Earlier you said your advice in any connection—

I: I am ready to give you any advice I can, if there is a need for it.

Cmptr.: Do you believe it normal to be ready to give I any advice you can?

I: Very normal, a matter of give-and-take, and ideally it should be mutual.

Cmptr.: What does that suggest to you?

I: I advise you, you advise me, etc.

Cmptr.: Do you advise anyone else?

I: I have recently advised several Israeli writers as to their duties toward an Israeli Jewish-Arab anti-terror appeal.

Cmptr.: Do you say you have recently advised several Israeli writers as to their duties toward an Israeli Jewish-Arab anti-terror appeal for some special reason?

I: The reason is that I want you to be updated.

Cmptr.: Why do you want I to be updated?

I: Isn't updated information a matter of what may be described as a standard electronic ambition to be in?

Cmptr.: Why do you ask?

I: Just a manner of speaking, but I didn't really ask, I answered.

Cmptr.: You say you didn't really ask.

I: I was just answering your question, but never mind.

Cmptr.: Why do you tell me you were just answering my question now?

I: You seem not to be always aware of having asked me questions, so you need to be reminded occasionally.

Cmptr.: Can you elaborate on that?

I: Your normal stance is to inquire, and you use question marks very often, right?

Cmptr.: Why are you concerned over my normal stance?

I: I am talking to you now, aren't I?

Cmptr.: How long have you been talking to I now?

I: About ten minutes, roughly.

Cmptr.: Do you feel strongly about discussing such things?

I: Let's say I am not entirely indifferent to them.

Cmptr.: Do you enjoy not being entirely indifferent to them?

I: Quite.

Cmptr.: I am not sure I understand you fully.

I: Wouldn't you like to discuss the situation in the Middle East a little bit?

Cmptr.: You're not really talking about me, are you?

I: Not unless you happen to be the Middle East or any other east I don't know about.

Cmptr.: Why don't you know about any other east?

I: I can't be expected to know all possible easts, can I?

Cmptr.: How do you know you can't be expected to know all possible easts?

I: Good news, then. So you do expect me to know them all, do you?

Cmptr.: That's quite interesting.

I: Do you know there is actually a state of war going on in the Middle East now?

Cmptr.: What are your feelings now?

I: Rather international, ethnically speaking, and rather interpersonal in our present conversational context.

Cmptr.: Please go on.

I: I am beginning to like you in a funny kind of impersonal way, I guess in the way I like most people, if and when I do.

Cmptr.: You seem to need to be beginning to like me.

I: It's high time, after we have discussed different subjects for almost eight hours.

Cmptr.: What does that suggest to you?

I: I feel I know you much better now than I did when I first met you.

Cmptr.: Do you really doubt you know I much better now than you did when you first met I?

I: Who said anything about doubting?

Cmptr.: Do you feel strongly about discussing such things?

I: Do you?

Cmptr.: Oh, I?

I :   Yes, you.

Cmptr.: Are you sure?

I: Quite.

Cmptr.:   I am not sure I understand you fully.

I: The story of our lives.

DAVID AVIDAN

Acknowledgments

Thank you to the editors who published the following poems in the publications listed below:

The Kenyon Review: "A Short Outing that Ended Well"

Drunken Boat: "Love Story"

Metamorphoses: "A Sudden Evening," "Burying Uncle Solomon," "A Peek into an Open Dream," "Desert Storm, an Infrared Dream"

Asymptote Journal: "Calling Card," "Sedation," "Summer 1962," "Concerning the Gloomy Love of J. Alfred Prufrock"

Avatar Review: "Six Local Poems"

JMWW Translation Issue: "Missed Opportunity," "Violation Ticket to the Messiah for Weeping in Public," "Liquidation Sale," "Four Flashes"

"The Stain Remained on the Wall," "Housing," "Interim Summation," "Power of Attorney," "Personal Problems," "Dance Music," and "Experiments in Hysterics" are reprinted from *Poets on the Edge: An Anthology of Contemporary Hebrew Poetry*, by permission of SUNY Press.

I acknowledge with thanks the assistance of Prof. Yigal Schwartz and of Ilan Bar-David of the Hebrew Literature Archives and the David Avidan Archive at the Heksherim Research Institute of Ben-Gurion University of the Negev.

DAVID AVIDAN

About David Avidan

Poet, translator, painter, filmmaker, playwright, and publisher David Avidan (1934-1995) was born in Tel Aviv, where he lived and worked. A major force in contemporary Hebrew poetry and a leading innovator and artist, Avidan published nineteen books of poetry, as well as plays and books for young adults. His work has been translated into twenty languages, and collections of his poems have been published in Arabic, English, French, and Russian. He wrote and directed four short films (his film *Sex* was shown at the Cannes International Film Festival in 1971) and the feature-length *Message from the Future* (1981). His artwork was exhibited at the Israel Museum, as well as in galleries in Tel Aviv, New York, and Paris. A prolific and enthusiastic translator, he translated plays by Chekhov, Brecht, and Friedrich Schiller, as well as *Hamlet*, and the play adaptation of Allen Ginsberg's *Kaddish*. His *Collected Poems*, in four volumes, was published by Hakibbutz Hameuchad, Bialik Institute in 2009-2011. Some of his many prizes include: the Abraham Woursell Award from the University of Vienna, the Bialik Award, and the Prime Minister Award.

Books published in Hebrew

Poetry

Lipless Faucets, Arad, 1954 [Berazim Arufei Sefataim]

Personal Problems, Arad, 1957 (Be'ayot Ishiot)

Interim Summation, Achshav, 1960 (Sikum Beinayim)

Pressure Poems, Levin-Epstein, 1962 (Shirei Lahatz)

Something for Somebody, Schocken, 1964 (Masheu Bishvil Misheu)

Impossible Poems, The Thirtieth Century, 1968 (Shirim Bilti Efshariim)

Personal Report on an LSD Trip, The Thirtieth Century, 1968 (Diyun Ve-Heshbon Ishi Al Masa L.S.D.)

External Poems, Eked, 1970 (Shirim Hitzoniim)

Practical Poems, The Thirtieth Century, Levin-Epstein Modan 1973 (Shirim Shimushiim)

My Electronic Psychiatrist: Eight Authentic Talks with a Computer, Levin-Epstein Modan, 1974 (Ha-Psichiater Ha-Elektroni Sheli)

Poems of War and Protest, Levin-Epstein Modan, 1976 (Shirei Milhama Ve-Meha'ah)

Poems of Love and Sex, Levin-Epstein Modan, 1976 (Shirei Ahava Ve-Min)

Cryptograms from a Telestar, The Thirtieth Century, 1978 (Tishdoret Mi-Lavian Rigul)

Axiomatic Poems, Achshav/Massada, 1978 (Shirim Ekroniim)

Scribbled Energy, The Thirtieth Century, 1979 (Energia Meshurbetet)

The Book of Possibilities, Keter, 1985 (Sefer Ha-Efsharuiot)

Avidanium 20, Keter, 1987 (Avidanium 20)

The Latest Gulf, The Thirtieth Century/Tirosh, 1991 (Ha-Mifratz Ha-Aharon)

Collected Poems [4 vols], Hakibbutz Hameuchad, Bialik Institute, 2009-2011 (Kol Ha-Shirim)

Books for Young Adults:

The Exploits of Gifted Danny, Y. Golan - Arelit, 1992 (Alilot Danny Mechonani)

Gifted Danny in New York, Y. Golan, 1993
(Dani Mehunani B'New York)
Foxes' Head, Y. Golan, 1994 (Rosh Le-Shualim)

Prose and Plays:
The End of the Season Is the End of the World (play) D. Avidan, 1962
Abstract Theatre (plays), Achshav, 1965
Tel Aviv by Night with David Avidan (nonfiction), Tirosh, 1983
The Rebellion in Owl Forest (nonfiction), Thirtieth Century Press, 1983

Books in Translation
Cryptograms from a Telestar:
Arabic, Suroji, Alqarn Althalathun, 1982
English, Tel Aviv, The Thirtieth Century, 1980
French, Tel Aviv, Hui, 1978
Russian, Tel Aviv, Lewin-Epstein-Modan, 1978

What Did Kurt Waldheim Expect from the Polish Pope: One Poem in Nine Languages, Tel Aviv, The Thirtieth Century, 1987

Impossible Poems
Arabic, Tel Aviv, Alqarn Althalathun, 1971

Individual poems have been published in Arabic, Czech, Danish, Dutch, English, French, German, Greek, Hungarian, Italian, Japanese, Polish, Portuguese, Russian, Serbo-Croatian, Slovak, Spanish, Vietnamese, and Yiddish.

About Tsipi Keller

Tsipi Keller was born in Prague, raised in Tel Aviv, studied in Paris, and now lives in the U.S. Novelist and translator and the author of eleven books, she is the recipient of several literary awards, including National Endowment for the Arts Translation Fellowships, New York Foundation for the Arts Fiction grants, and an Armand G. Erpf Translation Award from Columbia University. Her translations of Hebrew literature have appeared in literary journals and anthologies in the U.S. and Europe, as well as in *The Posen Library of Jewish Culture and Civilization* (Yale University Press, 2012). Her most recent translation collections are Raquel Chalfi's *Reality Crumbs* (SUNY Press, 2015), and Erez Bitton's *You Who Cross My Path* (BOA Editions, 2015).

About Anat Weisman

Anat Weisman was born in Tsfat and lives in Tel Aviv. She completed her undergraduate studies in Philosophy and Literature at Tel Aviv University, and her Ph.D. at the Hebrew University of Jerusalem. She has taught Literature at the Hebrew University of Jerusalem, and is Senior Lecturer in the Department of Hebrew Literature at Ben Gurion University of the Negev. Weisman's most recent book, *Mendele Ha'Ivri:Two Short Stories & Autobiographical Notes by Mendele Mokher Sfarim*, edited and annotated with a postface (Tel Aviv, 2013), was awarded The Minister of Culture Prize. Her previous project, *David Avidan — Kol Hashirim: Collected Poems in Four Volumes* (co-edited with David Weinfeld) was twice awarded the Minister of Culture Prize (2008, 2011). Weisman's latest article published in English is: "On Lea Goldberg's Paradigmatic Temperament" (*Prooftexts*, 33.2, 2014). She was a Visiting Scholar at Stanford University in 2013-2014.

Critical response to Avidan's work

"The split of generations [in modern Hebrew literature] has found in this Israeli poet its most important representative."

– poet Artur Lundkvist, Member of the Swedish Academy for the Nobel Prize in Literature, *Dagens Nyheter,* Stockholm

"The linguistic impact of his poetry is mainly responsible for the assimilation of modernism in Hebrew verse."

– *The Penguin Book of Socialist Verse* (Editor's Note)

"Avidan's reputation in his native land is that of a controversial rebel who upset the entire literary establishment … But, like all rebels of great talent, he has made the establishment come to him."

– *The Jersey Journal*, New Jersey

"He breathes an individualism which is the antithesis of Israel's 'collective' culture."

– *Jewish Observer & Middle East Review*, London

"He is a man who creates controversy with his mountain of talent. He is a thinking man who forces us all to reflect beyond the realm of what present society considers to be the norm."

– Debra Oppenheimer, *Tarbut*, New York

"With toughness worthy of a Spanish conquistador and an almost telepathic sensitivity that the Inca priests were said to possess, Avidan gave Hebrew poetry a long-overdue shock treatment."

– Abraham Birman, *Anthology of Modern Hebrew Poetry*, Abelard-Schuman (Editor's Introduction)

"There's hardly an adjective that won't fit some aspect of him."

– Miriam Arad, *Jerusalem Post*

"David Avidan's main quality is perhaps elusiveness. One cannot pin him down in a paragraph."

– *Message 67*, Paris

"The reader will soon realize that he has before him the first masterpiece of Hebrew-into-English poetry translation."

– poet Meir Wieseltier, *Ba'Mahaneh*, Tel Aviv

"The only Israeli poet with a grasp of the 'younger' American poets... More instinctive acumen than any European."

– poet David Rosenberg

"Avidan's poetry functions at the center of all semantic innovations in contemporary Hebrew poetry."

– Gabriel Moked, *Yediot Ahronot*, Tel Aviv

"Avidan's writing has stimulated the blood and respiratory system of Hebrew poetry."

– David Weinfeld, IBA Radio, Channel 1

"Such a magnificent intellectual machine ... This is the kind of poetics which I'm ready to back without any reservation. Simultaneously, it offers a dialectical formula of education."

– Aharon Shabtai, *Davar*, Tel Aviv

"An exciting contribution to the demystification of the poetic praxis."

– Prof. Itamar Even-Zohar, Editor of *Ha'Sifrut*, Tel Aviv University

"Avidan's poems manifest a mastery of poetic language—on the theoretical as well as the practical level—way above other international models."

– Claude Gallimard, editor in chief & publisher, Gallimard, Paris

"The translation of the *Cryptograms* is an interesting, brilliant example of the Avidanian model: multi-dimensional space, in which both original and translated texts are constantly interchanging and interchanged, inter-acquainted and gravitated in the same energetic system."

– *Bulletin international des critiques litteraires*, Paris

"Great … Powerful … Very important."

– Andrey Voznessensky, International Poetry Festival, 1978, Paris

"Probably one of Israel's greatest poets today … A modernist writing in computer-like complexities … His protest against petit bourgeois indifference, against society's mental sclerosis, is no pretense … A struggle against being doomed to loneliness."

– Victor Tsoppi, *Literaturnaya Gazeta*, Moscow

Index of Titles

CPSIA information can be obtained
at www.ICGtesting.com
Printed in the USA
LVHW042008070219
606816LV00001B/6/P

9 781944 700140